Who Owns You?

The Corporate Gold-Rush to Patent Your Genes

David Koepsell

WILEY-BLACKWELL

A John Wiley & Sons, Ltd., Publication

This edition first published 2009
© 2009 David Koepsell

Blackwell Publishing was acquired by John Wiley & Sons in February 2007. Blackwell's
publishing program has been merged with Wiley's global Scientific, Technical, and Medical
business to form Wiley-Blackwell.

Registered Office
John Wiley & Sons Ltd, The Atrium, Southern Gate, Chichester, West Sussex, PO19 8SQ,
United Kingdom

Editorial Offices
350 Main Street, Malden, MA 02148-5020, USA
9600 Garsington Road, Oxford, OX4 2DQ, UK
The Atrium, Southern Gate, Chichester, West Sussex, PO19 8SQ, UK

For details of our global editorial offices, for customer services, and for information about
how to apply for permission to reuse the copyright material in this book please see our
website at www.wiley.com/wiley-blackwell.

The right of David Koepsell to be identified as the author of this work has been asserted
in accordance with the Copyright, Designs and Patents Act 1988.

Wiley also publishes its books in a variety of electronic formats. Some content that
appears in print may not be available in electronic books.

Designations used by companies to distinguish their products are often claimed as
trademarks. All brand names and product names used in this book are trade names,
service marks, trademarks or registered trademarks of their respective owners. The
publisher is not associated with any product or vendor mentioned in this book. This
publication is designed to provide accurate and authoritative information in regard to the
subject matter covered. It is sold on the understanding that the publisher is not engaged in
rendering professional services. If professional advice or other expert assistance is required,
the services of a competent professional should be sought.

Library of Congress Cataloging-in-Publication Data

Koepsell, David R. (David Richard)
    Who owns you? : the corporate gold-rush to patent your genes / David Koepsell.
      p. cm. – (Blackwell public philosophy)
    Includes bibliographical references and index.
    ISBN 978-1-4051-8731-2 (hardcover : alk. paper) – ISBN 978-1-4051-8730-5 (pbk. : alk.
paper)
1. Genes–Patents.   2. Human genetics–Law and legislation.   3 Intellectual property–
Moral and ethical aspects.   4. Personality (Law)   I. Title.
  K1519.B54K64 2009
    346.04′86–dc22

                                                                            2008041638

A catalogue record for this book is available from the British Library.

Set in 10.5/13.5 pt Minion by SNP Best-set Typesetter Ltd., Hong Kong
Printed and bound in Malaysia by Vivar Printing Sdn Bhd
01   2009

Who Owns You?

Blackwell Public Philosophy

Edited by Michael Boylan, Marymount University

In a world of 24-hour news cycles and increasingly specialized knowledge, the Blackwell Public Philosophy series takes seriously the idea that there is a need and demand for engaging and thoughtful discussion of topics of broad public importance. Philosophy itself is historically grounded in the public square, bringing people together to try to understand the various issues that shape their lives and give them meaning. This "love of wisdom" – the essence of philosophy – lies at the heart of the series. Written in an accessible, jargon-free manner by internationally renowned authors, each book is an invitation to the world beyond newsflashes and soundbites and into public wisdom.

Permission to Steal: Revealing the Roots of Corporate Scandal by Lisa H. Newton
Doubting Darwin? Creationist Designs on Evolution by Sahotra Sarkar
The Extinction of Desire: A Tale of Enlightenment by Michael Boylan
Torture and the Ticking Bomb by Bob Brecher
In Defense of Dolphins: The New Moral Frontier by Thomas I. White
Terrorism and Counter-Terrorism: Ethics and Liberal Democracy by Seumas Miller

Forthcoming:
Spiritual but Not Religious: The Evolving Science of the Soul by Christian Erickson
Evil On-Line: Explorations of Evil and Wickedness on the Web by Dean Cocking and Jeroen
    van den Hoven

For further information about individual titles in the series, supplementary material, and regular updates, visit www.blackwellpublishing.com/publicphilosophy

To Vanessa

CONTENTS

Acknowledgements   ix

Introduction   1
1 Individual and Collective Rights in Genomic Data:
   Preliminary Issues   20
2 Ethics and Ontology: A Brief Discourse
   on Method   40
3 The Science: Genes and Phenotypes   49
4 DNA, Species, Individuals, and Persons   66
5 Legal Dimensions in Gene Ownership   83
6 Are Genes Intellectual Property?   101
7 DNA and The Commons   119
8 Pragmatic Considerations of Gene Ownership   137
9 So, Who Owns You?: Some Conclusions about Genes,
   Property, and Personhood   155

   Notes   171
   Index   181

ACKNOWLEDGEMENTS

I am grateful to the Yale Interdisciplinary Bioethics Center for appointing me as their Donaghue Initiative Fellow in Research Ethics, 2006–07. I drafted a significant portion of this book during that appointment, and had the chance to hash out many of these issues with the staff, affiliated faculty, and others who participated in events that year. Special thanks to all the good people at Yale including especially: Robert Levine, Julius Landwirth, Carol Pollard, Autumn Ridenour, and Jonathan Moser. Thanks also to the folks at the New Haven dog park for keeping Buttercup and me company during my residency at Yale. Many thanks to my wife Vanessa who gave me significant scientific guidance and lots of encouragement as I worked out these issues and drafted the book. My parents, Eva Hwa and Richard Koepsell provided commentary and feedback on early drafts of chapters and I am, as always, grateful for their continuing encouragement. My dear friend Peter Hare, who recently passed away, also kept me company, bought me lunches, and encouraged my work while at Yale . . . I am grateful for his guidance and friendship and will miss him dearly. Thanks to Barry Smith, who has remained a helpful and encouraging mentor as I pursue the sometimes frustrating, but often fruitful path of philosophy. Thank you also to Denise Riley who helped dig up obscure articles, and arranged almost all the research for my trip to Yale. Finally, many thanks to anyone I have forgotten, including all those who have given me probing questions, puzzling scenarios, and further guidance in the talks I have given on this fascinating subject over the past two years.

David Koepsell
Amherst, NY
March 25, 2008

INTRODUCTION

"Who owns you?" It seems an odd and dated question. Slavery, after all, has been universally outlawed, and while exploitation and pockets of indentured servitude, human trafficking, and other modern forms of slavery continue, it isn't a real concern for the majority of the human race, most especially those of you who can afford this book. You quite rightly need not fear being owned in the most traditional and reprehensible sense by which humans purchased, traded, and used other humans for labor over many millennia. So what's the fuss? No one owns me, so why should I care? Unfortunately, it's not so simple. New and more subtle forms of ownership have emerged in the past hundred years that now impact on essential qualities and features of each of us. When intellectual property laws were first conceived, the notion was to encourage the invention and authorship of useful and pleasing machines, devices, stories, music, and art. Now, thanks to creative interpretations and applications of patent laws, parts of living things can be owned. Patents have been issued, in surprisingly large numbers, on the essential building blocks of multiple life-forms, including humans – including you.

You and Your Genes

Before we begin to explore the ways in which patents are being used to claim rights over genes (which are parts of you), let's spend a little time getting to know what a gene is, and how genes relate to you, the species, and every other living thing. There's a more in-depth scientific discussion of genes in Chapter 3, so this will be just a very superficial introduction to get us into the topic, and then we'll begin discussing the implications of gene patents ethically, socially, and politically.

All living things are composed of complex molecules called proteins, as well as other "organic" (meaning carbon-based) molecules. The instructions for building all of these molecules, and putting them together in the form they are in (as bacteria, monkeys, or elephants, for instance) are encoded in one very complex type of molecule typically known as deoxyribonucleic acid or DNA. We are all pretty much familiar with the depiction of the famous structure of DNA as a double helix, and many are familiar with the drama of that discovery by the scientists Francis Crick, James Watson, and their lesser-known but equally important colleagues Rosalind Franklin and Maurice Wilkins. In sum, DNA encodes the information used by the cells of every living thing to make it grow as it does and live as it does.[1]

We are still in the midst of deciphering the complex code of DNA. Scientists are attempting to understand how certain parts of the code are responsible for our individual traits and characteristics, such as eye color, height, appearance, propensities for diseases, and genetic or hereditary diseases themselves. Human DNA has roughly three billion single elements, and we can think of each one of these three billion for now as a digit, or like a "bit" in computer code – the smallest unit of useful information in the code. Except, in DNA, each bit can have one of four different values (A, C, T, or G, standing for the four amino acids involved: adenine, cytosine, thymine, and guanine) whereas in binary computer code, bits are only "0" or "1." Like subroutines in computer code, strings within the three billion "base pairs" cause certain things to happen in methodical, determinable ways. One of the best understood "subroutines" is what we call a "gene." For decades, scientists have labored under the working hypothesis that "each gene codes a protein," which means that there are recognizable substrings within the DNA that cause cells to make specific proteins. Thus, for instance, there is a gene that causes the eyes of all color-sighted animals to grow and maintain functioning cones that enable all of those creatures to view things in color. The gene responsible is shared among all color-sighted humans, as well as all known color-sighted creatures in general, from fruit flies to elephants. Scientists still work under the presumption that every single element of our development and ongoing metabolism is largely directed and maintained by information in certain genes. So, for example, there's a gene for brown eyes, for producing lactase (which digests milk products), for growing knee-caps.

Scientists are discovering that the one-gene, one-protein hypothesis may be an oversimplification, and that the information that directs all of the complex development and functioning of an organism may also come in other useful units. Back in the 1980s and 1990s, a huge multinational science project was created to develop a road-map of sorts for the three-billion base pair code in human DNA. The Human Genome Project (HGP) aimed at "mapping" human DNA, and thus showing where the useful bits, conceived of as being genes, appeared in that long string of information. At the start of the HGP, scientists expected to find about 100,000 distinct human genes, but at its conclusion the number found was less than a third of that. It actually takes nearly 25,000 distinct genes to make a human. Many now believe that there are other useful ways that DNA stores and uses information, including in elements as short as a single base pair (a single-nucleotide polymorphism, or SNP) as well as larger chunks of genes that get shuffled or rearranged differently among individuals who share that gene. As well, many individual genes appear more than once in the whole genome (that three-billion base pair long sequence) and the number of times and places where that individual gene occurs, its "copy-number variation (CNV)," also seems to convey useful information that directs differentiation, development, and metabolism.[2]

The HGP launched in its wake several other efforts to decipher the relation of the string of the whole genome to the information it encodes, the environment, and finally the phenotype, or the physical instances of each and every individual human. Your "phenotype" is the structure of your body and all its parts, including organs, tissues, metabolism, etc. Your "genotype" is the string of base pairs of your DNA, its complete structure that contributes significantly to your phenotype. One of these efforts was the HapMap Project, meant to map out the places of individual variation among individual human genomes. Another one of these is the CNV Map Project, which will capture the full range of copy number variations, and their roles in phenotypic differences. The ultimate goal of producing all of these maps is a full understanding of all the means by which information is encoded in our genome, and how that information directs and maintains development and metabolism. A full understanding of the genome and its relationship to the environment and the organism will provide us ultimately with powerful new means of treatment of a variety of diseases, both inherited and environmental. Of course, the promise of deciphering all this information, and curing diseases, is attractive scientifically, morally, and also commercially. There's been a land-rush of sorts going on over the various maps of the human genome (and other genomes of other creatures too) and the stakes of the claims being made are patents. Patents over genes and other parts of the genome are the highly prized and incredibly valuable end-points for many of those parties who are bridging the pure scientific research on the genome with commercialization. The result is that parts of you, and every other living human being, are now patented.[3]

Your Patented Parts

Yes, parts of you are patented. Not your knee, not your femur, nor even your kidneys or spleen, but *the building blocks* of some of these and other parts, processes, or functions of every human being (and many other species, as we'll see) are now claimed under the right of patent by universities, corporations, individuals and other researchers as their property. This is what a patent represents. It represents a government-granted monopoly to exploit an invention exclusively over the rights of all others.

Let's consider that and what it means to you, to others, to scientists, and to the institution of science. When patents are granted, they give to the inventor (or whomever files for the patent and holds it) the exclusive right against all others to produce, reproduce or sell a product, or employ a process. So Pfizer, the company that owned the patent on Sertraline hydrochloride, or Zoloft™ as it's known on the market, had the exclusive right to synthesize and market that chemical as well as the exclusive use of whatever original processes it developed to synthesize it. It was a very profitable property right for Pfizer before the patent expired, as the drug has numerous uses and is widely prescribed. Others could potentially synthesize the drug themselves, but could never profit from its sale. This is why it is such a big deal when a patent on a pharmaceutical expires: others can synthesize it and profit from its sale when the drug goes "generic," as has happened with Zoloft™. The government-sponsored monopoly awarded by a patent is valuable, giving an exclusive right against all others over the thing patented, and all copies of that thing.

Imagine, for instance, that you are the inventor of the bicycle, and that when invented nothing remotely "bicycle-like" has ever existed. Because your invention is novel, non-obvious, and useful, the government gives to you the right to produce all bicycles in the United States (and thanks to various treaties, other parts of the world) for a period of time. That period of time has been extended over the past couple of decades from 17 to 20 years. So for the next 20 years, you can profit from *every* bicycle sold in the US.

The monopoly over a patented object constitutes a right to profit, but it also involves a loss of rights for others. Others may purchase your invention, they may take any individual one apart, or learn about its functioning (aided of course by the fact that the patent filing has made publicly available much of the object's methods, processes, and construction), but no one may construct your invention without paying royalties, and especially not if they do so intending to enter it into the stream of commerce. The patent system strikes a bargain in order to spur innovation and invention, and to also benefit the public by moving inventions ultimately into the "public domain." This bargain is supposed to provide an incentive for innovators to invest time and money into inventing new and useful things, bringing them to the marketplace with the protection of patents, and then in return, enriching society by making available to all the technique and technology utilized by the original inventor, and making it all free and open to all to use and continue to improve upon when the patent expires.

Make no mistake about it, the patent monopoly is strong. The only thing you have to demonstrate once you've successfully been granted a patent is that some other invention is substantially the same thing as the one you patented and then you can sue the late-comer, get damages for lost profits, and keep them from making and marketing their infringing product for the rest of the term of your patent. Your filing of the patent first is prima facie proof of your ownership of the invention, and the late-comer, no matter what his or her intention, must yield to you in the market. You own that swath of intellectual property. No one may infringe upon it without paying you some royalty.

Owning a patent doesn't grant you exclusive rights over the uses of each instance of your invention, nor to possess any instance of it, nor to reclaim any of those that have entered the stream of commerce. While it is a strong right, it is limited in certain ways. It is not a possessory right. It is a right to fees or royalties. It is also limited in time. After twenty years the invention becomes part of the "public domain" and anyone may make copies of your invention without paying you any royalties. They may even make improvements and try to patent those improvements. So, the sense in which the thing patented is "owned" is very different from the way that other sorts of things are owned. Again, let's consider the original bicycle that you patented, and marketed. I might buy one of these bicycles, and I would properly be said to own that bicycle against all other claims. No one may deprive me of that particular bicycle, and I may do what I will with the physical object. I may ride it, sell it, or even tear it apart piece by piece and try to understand its workings. What I cannot legally do is assemble another one using it as a model, or even worse – sell the new one. You as the patent owner have this amount of control over me and no more, but this is plenty. While you are the patent holder you have an absolute monopoly over the creation of any new instances of the thing patented.

You may well wonder how patents came to be granted to genes when they seem so unlike bicycles. Genes are seemingly not "invented," nor assembled, nor packaged, nor sold like any other patentable thing. Which innovative acts are rewarded by granting a patent? The US Patent and Trademark Office (PTO) views the "isolation and purification" of genes as sufficiently innovative, inventive, and novel to warrant patent protection. What this means simply is that scientists who discover the beginning and end points of the string of base pairs constituting a particular gene, and delineate those points, weeding out extraneous bits that don't contribute to the functioning of that gene, have done enough in the eyes of the PTO to warrant a monopoly right to that gene. In an opinion issued in 2001, the PTO issued "more stringent" criteria for patent applications for genes, requiring a specific "utility" claim (all patents must be for "useful" things), which could be met simply by a statement of a "single specific, substantial, and credible" use such as the ability "to produce a useful protein or if it hybridizes near or serves as a marker for a disease gene."[4] We will discuss at length in the chapters that follow whether and how the current criteria might run afoul of the Patent Act's historical requirements, and if indeed the utility requirement is properly met by this new, more "stringent" hurdle, but for now, let's consider some real present effects of gene patents. What does the owner of a gene really possess, and why should we be concerned? To answer this, let's step back a bit and look first at some hypothetical scenarios, and then look at some real world issues that have arisen out of gene patents.

The "I, Robot, Your Robot" Scenario

Some might object to the claim that human gene patents have any real-world implications for ordinary people, and that the ownership rights granted by patents do nothing to impede our day-to-day existence, or any presumed human rights. This claim isn't entirely true, and the following analogy shows how:

Imagine that you are a robot. You are an artificially created android, running algorithms written by an inventor, and your parts are all the products of the same inventor. Assume that in these enlightened times robots are free. They are not enslaved and used for labor, but rather treated as equal beings with humans, entitled to the full panoply of human and civil rights. They can make their own decisions, go about their daily lives unencumbered by any special laws or restrictions. You are thus a free agent, pursuing your own life choices, including getting an education, pursuing hobbies, maybe even falling in robot love with another robot. It is still within 20 years of your invention, and the patents on you are all still in effect. But so what?

The fact that parts of you are patented has real repercussions for some of your life choices. Simply put, there are certain things you cannot do with or to yourself, and certain things you cannot do in the world without violating your patents. You cannot, for instance, try to improve upon the algorithms that comprise your personality, behaviors, movements, appearances, or any of your algorithms for that matter, without risking a lawsuit. In the US at least, patents prevent others not just from making or commercially exploiting the thing patented, but also restrict others from doing "research" on the thing patented other than "purely philosophical" research. Thus, poking around in "your" algorithms, especially with the intent to modify them (for instance, to make you think better, run faster, be stronger) may very well infringe your inventor's patents. If you wanted to improve yourself, you'd need to pay royalties to the original patent holder on any improvement patent you would then have to file on yourself. You would be even more likely to be sued if you tried to reproduce some part of yourself, or all of yourself, without seeking a license to do so from your creator.

As a robot, of course, you cannot reproduce sexually. Fortunately (or unfortunately if you worry about robot privacy rights) all your innovative parts and processes have been laid bare by the patents on file with the PTO. Moreover, you can deconstruct your physical self, see how you fit together, and theoretically make your offspring piece by piece in your own image. Unfortunately, this would be an unauthorized reproduction and you could get sued for patent infringement. So in what sense are you "your own" robot, and in what sense are you still partly owned by your inventor? Certainly, your rights over yourself are less than those of the inventor's rights over his own body and its products. A non-patented being can modify, reproduce, and generally muck about with his own body, mind, and functioning without risking a patent suit.

Are these significant limitations on freedom? Obviously, that depends on what you think about the rights you feel you possess over your own body and its products. It does not rise to the level of slavery, but certainly the right to reproduce is one most people feel strongly about and would not want curtailed. Imagine paying royalties to have a child.

But it could never come to that with humans, could it? There are some considerable differences between humans and robots, not least of which is that no human (yet) has been the product of another human's invention. But this difference has become meaningless, as we shall see, under current interpretations of the patent law that have allowed for the patenting of genes, whether invented (as we have traditionally used the term) or not. Before we get into that long discussion, which will occupy a fair amount of this book, let's first consider another historical scenario which touches upon traditionally held notions of privacy and bodily autonomy, and then analyze some real world issues that gene patents presently create.

The Elephant Man Scenario

Joseph Merrick (not John, as he has erroneously been called by most) suffered from a disfiguring disease and lived a hobbled and at times miserable life because of the disease. Moreover, he was clearly exploited by some, set upon a freak-show stage, and used as a means of income, enriching others at the expense of his dignity. Joseph Merrick, known as the "Elephant Man," was not responsible for his condition. Nature was. Through what was likely a genetic disease, he grew excess tissue and bone all over his body, resulting in a crippling deformity that has been much celebrated since then in various media. In the Victorian era, natural wonders were very much in vogue, and when he was discovered by the surgeon Frederick Treves, Joseph Merrick became an instant sensation among England's upper crust. While he had started his life as a freak on display, he ended as a gentleman, of sorts, cared for, housed, clothed, and fed by his Victorian benefactors. Treves was knighted, and Merrick died in 1890 at the age of 27.[5]

Merrick's bones, until recently, were on display at the Royal London Hospital museum, but there is no evidence that Merrick gave consent to give his body to science. In his death, his interest to science was simply made use of with no apparent or expressed consent by him. His life, memory, and now bones are the subject of numerous works of both fiction and nonfiction based in whole or in part upon Joseph Merrick and his unfortunate malady. While he lived, he received not compensation but care in return for his role as a deformed person in Queen Victoria's Court. He was a curiosity at all times, earning money first for the hawkers who ran the freak-show, and then earning respect, fame, scholarly accolades, and a knighthood for Treves. Despite popular lore otherwise, there is no evidence either for physical abuse at the hands of either the hawkers nor Treves. Moreover, fulfilling these roles was Merrick's only possible means of support given his condition. And yet, we wonder, while others grew wealthy or famous off Merrick's life, and others have grown wealthy and famous off his memory and story, where is Merrick's share? Is there something fundamentally unfair in the use of a person's accidental condition for another's enrichment?

Setting aside issues of property and ownership, something about the use of Merrick for the aggrandizement or enrichment of others strikes us as wrong. Putting ourselves in his shoes, we must wonder how we would feel. Would we feel exploited? Would we wish for some greater share of the riches and fame? Do we sense that Merrick was owed something more? Accidents of nature notwithstanding, we feel a certain inherent right over our bodies and the use of ourselves, excluding others from enjoyment or profit at our expense without our explicit consent. Even though we are not the products of our own intention (at least not until we begin to physically alter ourselves), there is a sense that we should be able to direct our uses intentionally to the exclusion of all others. The practice of bio-prospecting, by which scientists and pharmaceutical companies profit from discoveries of biological accidents in individuals and populations (typically geographically isolated, and often quite poor) is very much like the relationship between Treves and Merrick. Taking our intuitions about the justice of Merrick's exploitation into account, and setting aside hypothetical scenarios for the moment, let's look at how bio-prospecting and gene-mining are earning profits for some, and potentially exploiting certain individuals and populations in the real world.

There's Gold in Them Thar Genes! Bio-Prospecting and Social Justice

"Bio-prospecting" is the derogatory term given to the practice of looking for profitable and useful materials in nature and then staking a property claim, usually under patents, over some element of the discovery. Of course, humans have long exploited the natural world for profit, taking resources and utilizing them, breeding new hybrids, and reaping the profits. Until recently, however, the profits were made at the supply side, by generating surpluses, and entering the marketplace with increased efficiency. Only within the last 50 years have profits begun to be made not solely by increased production and surplus supply (of "tokens," or individual objects – like hundreds of thousands of identical, well-made chairs, for instance), but rather by claiming rights over the "types" of objects themselves – the universal *form* of the item marketed and sold. It is the difference between making money by growing and harvesting apples, and making money by claiming rights to *all* apples and collecting royalties on all apples sold, whether you planted and harvested them or not.

Perhaps one of the most famous cases of alleged bio-prospecting, also sometimes called bio-piracy, involves the Neem tree of India. The Neem tree has an ancient history in Indian traditional medicine, but in the mid 1990s the US Department of Agriculture and a private pharmaceutical company sought to patent the process of extracting a natural compound found in the Neem tree, *azadirachtin*, to vocal objections from the Indian government and some not-for-profit organizations. The compound had a significant use as a pesticide, but the Indian government claimed that this was long-held traditional knowledge in India, pre-dating the "invention" of this use by those who sought suddenly to patent it.[6] Ordinarily, patents can only be granted for new, non-obvious and useful inventions, but in this case there was nothing new nor non-obvious about this product's use as a pesticide. Eventually, the patent was overturned, but it raised public consciousness about the growing practice of bio-prospecting, as well as the potential for finding and exploiting useful natural compounds in the oceans and rainforests. This is now the motivating impulse behind Craig Venter's recent work, scouring the oceans looking for unknown organisms that could be beneficial in drug development.[7] We'll talk more about Dr Venter in later chapters, but let's focus now on the practice of bio-prospecting, what it means for the institution of patenting, and its implications for developing countries.

Discovery, not Invention

Until recently, patents were limited to inventions, and discoveries were not afforded that right. The purpose, after all, of the institution of patenting is to encourage innovation, not discovery. Discovery is the realm of science, whereas patenting is the reward of technological innovation – of the creation of new, non-obvious, and useful (words used in the Patent Act) things that generally enter the stream of commerce. Some notable exceptions to this might seem to have existed in the form of "plant patents." They could be granted to anyone who invented or "discovered" and asexually reproduced any "*distinct, new* variety of plant, including cultivated sports, mutants, hybrids, and newly found seedlings, other than a tuber-propagated plant or a plant found in an uncultivated state." Plant patents still require innovation – some alteration of the natural world and a bending of it to human will.

Over the course of the last 30 years, the extent of patentable life-forms has slowly grown. As we will see in more depth later, the first patents on non-plant life-forms began to be issued in 1980, with the case of *Chakrabarty*, discussed at more length later. The rationale for granting these patents has been that the patented life-forms were genetically engineered. Because they did not occur in nature, and were the products of human innovation and intention, and were non-obvious, new, and useful, they were considered properly patentable. Examples of patentable life-forms have included: petroleum eating bacteria, mono-clonal genetically engineered bacteria used to produce insulin, human growth hormone, and other rather useful creations not of nature, but of man.

More contentious, and clearly pushing the edge of the envelope of patent law, have been patents that seem to have been issued not for inventions, but for bare discoveries. Examples include disease-gene patents, such as a recent one issued to the discoverers of the gene for Canavan's disease. In 1997, the Miami Children's Hospital obtained a license for a DNA sample from human subjects of research aimed at discovering the genetic source of Canavan's disease, a malady afflicting 1 in 6400 Ashkenazi Jewish children, and caused by a mutation on chromosome 17. The presence of the gene leads to a deficiency of the enzyme aspartoacylase, gradually destroy-ing the central nervous system and killing the sufferer. The Miami Chil-dren's Hospital applied for and obtained a patent for the gene that causes the disease, and now anyone wishing to develop or sell tests for that disease must pay royalties to the hospital. Bitter disputes erupted over the owner-ship, licensing, and profits flowing from the patent, with parents whose afflicted children's tissues were used in the discovery of the gene angrily seeking some compensation. A lawsuit was settled for an undisclosed sum in 2003.[8]

The Miami Children's Hospital Case underscores the emerging conflicts among science, cultural or ethnic interests, and commerce. These conflicts will continue and grow as the trend of searching for and exploiting genetic homogeneity in populations proves valuable in gene discovery and phar-maceutical manufacture.

Genetic Diversity and Cultural Commons

Genetic disease discovery has been aided by the fact that certain popula-tions have been historically isolated and therefore more genetically homo-geneous than others. Whether because of cultural or geographic pressures, certain groups have remained more inbred than others (meaning that genetically related individuals breed more frequently with one another than in more heterogeneous populations), thus preserving and enhancing cer-tain genetic traits, and also increasing the prevalence of certain genetic diseases. Canavan's disease, mentioned above, and Tay-Sachs are examples of diseases more common to Ashkenazi Jews than to some other ethnic groups. Geographically isolated populations also pose a ripe potential pool for discovery of other genetic diseases or traits that might be useful in developing pharmaceuticals or tests for diseases.

It is potentially profitable to scour as many different genomes as possi-ble, searching for interesting and useful genetic diversity. That diversity helps scientists to trace the origins of genetic diseases and inherent immu-nities that might be commercialized through new medications or treat-ments. Many genetically isolated populations are now potentially valuable treasure-troves for profitable genetic discoveries. The scientific value of researching geographically or culturally isolated genetic subgroups goes back decades, but the potential commercial value, and recent corporate forays into the rainforests, savannahs, and island populations for commercial gene discovery, has resulted in a sort of backlash. Various not-for-profit organizations have begun to try to educate native populations, and to push for greater bargaining power, royalties, or rights for less-developed populations who might be "taken advantage of" in the process of commercially-motivated gene discovery.[9] Others have coordinated themselves to develop commercially beneficial uses of their genetic resources, essentially taking control of the market for their own genes.[10]

Others have argued that the human genome is simply not an appropriate landscape for staking out monopolistic claims, and that the resource of human DNA is one held in common by all humans. Aside from the legal arguments that have been made rejecting the patentability of a raw product of nature, many wonder about the ethical implications of affording some monopolistic control over the information that can be found in the genes of all or some of us without any necessity for remuneration of donors or "holders" of the commercialized genes for the profits that information affords. Why shouldn't underprivileged populations whose genes help us find new cures profit somehow for their contribution to human knowledge? Why shouldn't the human population as a whole reap some reward from the collective resource we share when science leads to profits? Just as we expect those who utilize other publicly-held commons to pay for their use of that resource through taxes or fees, or through some licensing or other regulatory framework, shouldn't we expect the same from those who are reaping profits from the use of genes that are, after all, part of each of us in common?

Are You Your Genes?

I have spoken to hundreds of people about the current situation in which more than one-fifth of human genes have been patented. An almost universal reaction has been one of initial puzzlement, followed by understanding, then outrage. How is it possible that our common genetic material is owned for the benefit of a few individuals or a corporation, without most people even knowing that this is the case? Many people have a visceral response – one of having been *violated*. Their genes are what make them who they are at a fundamental level. Most people sense that the ownership of that information, the stuff that makes them unique, should not be permitted. Of course, it's not quite like that. No one owns any *one* person's genes wholly (unless one of the few people who have conducted a full genotyping of themselves decides to try to patent his or her whole genome) and what makes us who we are is much more than our genes. Nonetheless, we feel strongly that the information that *helps* make us who we are at least in some large part, ought to be ours just as our own bodies and organs seem to be clearly ours.

However, the law and ethics of ownership over ourselves is not so clear-cut, and our intuitive sense of self-ownership is not reflected in the present law of organs or bodies. It ought not to be so surprising that the law of ownership over the genome or genes is even less clearly established and is in a turbulent state. In many ways, it seems like the Wild West. Claims are being staked out, and it's just a matter of time before a shoot-out ensues. What is clear is that our instincts about our self-ownership of our bodies and the information that makes them up is not in sync with the present patent law.

Setting aside the legal issues involved, we ought to perhaps pay some heed to our instincts. What is it about our individuality that is captured by our genes? That's a genuine, scientifically interesting, and potentially useful question that we are seeking answers for through the various gene mapping projects. A complete understanding of the relations among genes, genomes, haplotypes (closely linked genetic markers, often used to identify genetic traits or diseases), SNPs, CNVs and the environment would allow us to make more accurate predictions about the development of any individual organism. It would enable us to predict our potential for developing diseases and we could adjust our behaviors to help avoid certain fates due to genetic predispositions. We could strive to prevent diseases before they occur, or screen them out among selected embryos, or cure them in living organisms. Many are also aware of the potential for abuse, and the dangers of a lack of sufficient privacy over our individual genetic makeup. The *Gattaca*[11] scenario motivates many to be wary of the exposure of their genetic makeup to either commercial or scientific exploitation, and to consider carefully the relations between themselves and their genes. In the movie *Gattaca*, personal genetic information becomes easily analyzable, and of course the government puts it to use in ways that make us feel squeamish about the future of the technology. Parents are able to select traits with great precision when deciding to have a child, and naturally they choose those traits that society tends to value highly, such as physical strength, intelligence, and beauty. Those who, for some reason, have not been scientifically selected become part of a genetic sub-class, unable to enjoy many of the luxuries or benefits of a more genetically perfect society. Genetic surveillance is also commonplace in this dystopian near-future and is a real ethical concern for us as the technology to cheaply and easily screen DNA becomes ubiquitous.

Many people have come to believe that our future development is "all in our genes" and that the *Gattaca* future could somehow become a reality. Scientists are learning that genes are not completely deterministic, and that the environment plays a significant role in making us who we are, but the role and potential of genes as a source of important knowledge about us as individuals still stirs concern for many, and rightly so. While genes are not completely deterministic, there are some who are very interested in using genetic information to make important determinations. Consider the growth in the role of collecting genetic samples in criminal cases. Consider also the potential for coupling databanks of genetic materials gathered in criminal cases with an increased knowledge of the role of genes in certain mental illnesses. For instance, what if a genetic marker is found for a propensity toward pedophilia or other socially unacceptable or criminal behaviors? Shouldn't that information be used to screen for, and prevent criminals (or others whose genetic predispositions to certain diseases are known) from ever committing a crime? Insurers would also benefit by knowing who among us is predisposed to certain conditions, or who may be carrying latent genetic diseases. Even where the notion of self-ownership of our genes might not be fully logical (as we discuss later), many feel that privacy rights ought to protect us, and prevent the use of our genes by others for individual profit. We are at least the *custodians* of our own unique genes, aren't we? While no one *is* their genes, we have a sense that our genes are something important to us individually, and ought somehow to remain solely *our* business, rather than a resource for individual or collective profit. Do privacy rights protect our genetic information and should those rights trump the rights afforded by patent protection?

Genes, Information, and Privacy

There is tremendous and growing diversity in forms of legal and cultural protection of genetic information. The United States and Britain have been very liberal in affording governments and researchers use and even ownership of genetic information. Both countries are exploring the use of biometric information, including genetic information, for use at border crossings to enhance security. Because biometric information is difficult to fabricate, genetic "fingerprinting" promises to even more closely identify individuals than traditional fingerprinting technologies. Your genes, while they may not *be identical* with you, certainly do help to *identify* you. Different cultures have differing notions about privacy and their citizens' rights to not be identified, or to not have their identities used in some manner for the benefit of another.[12]

Consider, for instance, your image. Many of us believe that control of the use of our image or likeness is ours exclusively. In fact, in the United States, one's likeness is rather strictly believed both legally and culturally to be a matter of individual privacy and rights. Your image generally cannot be used for the profit of another without your express permission. Even in the current age of "reality" shows and live-blogging of our daily lives, individuals must typically grant permission for their image to be used for the profit of another. Even cautious not-for-profit users of images typically garner "waivers" from their subjects in case later someone decides to sue for improper use of their face or likeness. There seems to be a certain irony over the fact that it appears that we have greater protection for the use of our image than over the genetic information that helps to give us our appearances.

This is not the case in much of Europe, where culturally and politically there is greater respect for genetic privacy. We might well question the philosophical, cultural and legal assumptions behind varying degrees of privacy afforded to individuals and their genetic information, and compare that with other forms of privacy protection over things like likenesses, images, and biographies. Do we sense there is a significant difference between the sort of invasion we might feel exists when someone snaps our photo and uses it on an advertisement without our permission, and someone conceivably following us around with a vacuum cleaner, gathering our stray cells to use our DNA to possibly create a new blockbuster pharmaceutical? Are these analogous in any important way? If so, why is one not forbidden legally? A full analysis of the implications of gene patents ought to consider in-depth the possibility that there is a right to genetic privacy, and weigh those potential rights against the legal institution of patent.

The emergence of new abilities to scan and record our genetic makeup raises potential new claims to privacy invasions that were never conceived at the time the first act of those invasions occurred. Bio-banks abound with samples of tissues taken long before donors might have considered the possibility that someone, sometime in the future, might not only scan their tissues' genetic composition, but also possibly use that information for profit. This new technology, and the possibility for intrusions that were never properly contemplated, might cause us to consider creating new privacy rights. We have carved out new zones of privacy before, shrinking the realm of public or government interference in our private lives, and expanding the realm of personal space in the process.

Genes might be part of a newly recognized zone of privacy, at least to the extent that they are unique to us as individuals. Our individual genomes might deserve some sort of protection never previously necessary, and thus never previously protected. This could be the time to explore expanding once again our privacy laws as some nations have already done. Some legislators agree and the "Genetic Information Nondiscrimination Act (GINA)," H.R. 493, was passed on January 16, 2008 in the US Congress forbidding the use of genetic information for health insurance purposes, or for hiring or firing decisions in employment. This bill has since been signed into law, and the time seems ripe not just for philosophical musing about the implications discussed below, but for public policy action like that taken by representative Slaughter in drafting the GINA bill.

Practical Considerations: Gene Patents and Innovation

The coming century really will be one of revolutionary biotechnology. As much as the industrial revolution of the nineteenth century and the computer revolution of the twentieth century shifted our cultural landscape dramatically, the coming understanding of DNA will likely revolutionize numerous aspects of our society. It will impact commerce, health, privacy, law, and require significant ethical introspection. Our daily lives will also change as DNA and our individual genomes become important to us as information, potential commodities, and life-saving tools. We will have the power to transform our world at the molecular level, and alter our relationships with each other and our environments as well as with future generations. In the meantime, patenting genes poses a number of real-world, practical challenges with which we ought now to begin coming to grips. These aren't simply science fiction scenarios to ponder philosophically; there are immediate concerns that are posed by the current state of the law regarding patenting genes.

If genetic technology is to achieve its full promise and potential, we should carefully consider the effects of legal regulations on innovation. I have argued extensively in my first book and subsequently that intellectual property laws are not universally encouraging for innovation.[13] Sometimes they may stifle scientific inquiry and technological progress. The intellectual property regime we currently live under is relatively new, and there is no doubt that it has largely coincided with tremendous growth in both science and industry. The bargain between the public good and private innovators likely encourages a great deal of technological progress. But all bargains require balance, and at some point it is possible we went too far in favoring the rights of innovators over the necessity for public good. Intellectual property laws have changed over the past hundred years, shifting their focus away from moving innovations into the public domain, and developing more lengthy periods of profits for individual and corporate patent holders.

A number of scientists have expressed concern that patents on genes hinder science. This happens because once one party owns the patent on a gene, researchers study that gene at their own risk. If that gene is already staked out and patented, then any science that leads to invention regarding that gene would have to be licensed from the patent holder. Even investigating that gene, using tests that help find it, or markers used in experiments, may grow more expensive as fees for those products go up with the cost and profit of patenting. Patents can have a chilling effect as each new potential area for study must now be thoroughly researched not just within the scientific literature, but also through a patent search to see who owns what parts of the segment of the genome one wishes to study.

We should ask not only whether and how patents might be appropriate for genes, but in what ways patents might encourage or stifle science and spin-off technologies. Setting aside ethical, metaphysical, and legal questions, patents are affecting science in the real world, and if we are to keep the current patent system, we ought to ask whether it is meeting the purposes to which it was originally conceived, and whether genes are an economically efficient or practical subject for patents in general.

The Road Ahead

It may seem too late to inquire into the ethics, metaphysics, and public policy implications of gene patents when more than one-fifth of the human genome has already been patented and genes throughout the natural world are being mined for potential wealth right now. But more than once, public policies have been forced to evolve, change, or be scrapped entirely in the face of growing public awareness, debate, or intellectual and cultural paradigm shifts. While not comparable in scale to debates over civil rights leading to the abolition of slavery, or the civil rights laws of the 1960s, the problem of gene patenting does pose significant ethical, economic, and scientific concerns. Perhaps we cannot solve all of these problems, but a more publicly visible dialogue is in order.

At the heart of the debate are some fundamental questions that require philosophical analysis, but much more of the debate involves commonly held ethical assumptions about the nature of identity, and scientific questions regarding the role of genes in creating that identity. We will need to look into the relations of genes to species and individuals, as well as the nature of property rights over our bodies, parts of our bodies, and the information that makes our bodies grow and function. We will inquire into the present state of the law of patenting genes, as well as into issues of privacy in our bodily tissues and their products. And finally, we will examine the practical results of the current system of gene patenting, their ethical and economic consequences, and explore some potential new paradigms that might serve the dual purposes of encouraging innovation and serving the public good.

I hope this leads to further debate, and I expect that some of the things I propose in the pages to come will be controversial. What is important is to get this discussion out in the open, encourage those who make public policy to reconsider the current state of affairs, and perhaps develop some common agreement about how we ought to perceive and treat our genes ethically, legally, and scientifically as the biological age blossoms over the coming decades.

INDIVIDUAL AND COLLECTIVE RIGHTS IN GENOMIC DATA

PRELIMINARY ISSUES

Life on earth is bound together by a common heritage, centered around a molecule that is present in almost every living cell of every living creature. Deoxyribonucleic acid (DNA), composed of four base pairs, the amino acids thymine, adenine, cytosine, and guanine, encodes the data that directs, in conjunction with the environment, the development and metabolism of all nondependent living creatures. (There are ribonucleic acid (RNA)-based viruses and phages, but these are dependent upon other living creatures for their development and propagation.) DNA is composed of genes, each of which is a segment of an organism's DNA (which for humans is 3 billion base pairs long). Each gene does something specific, encoding the instructions for a cell's creation of a protein or enzyme, which in turn is responsible for cell differentiation, development, and reproduction. The mechanisms are now well understood. We know what DNA does in a very basic sense. The task that science is now completing is developing a full understanding of the relation and role of each gene, and other information encoded in DNA, to the development, functioning, and reproduction of the whole organism. The human genome is of course the one that interests us most, and understanding the role of each gene in causing us to grow and function as we do will afford us greater prediction and control over human health.

The first stage of that degree of understanding was *mapping* the genome. Once we know where each individual gene falls on the 3 billion base pair chain, we can start to understand differences among individuals and how they relate to the health and particular characteristics of each organism. The Human Genome Project (HGP) began in the early 1990s as a publicly-funded, international project to develop that essential map. Along the way, something happened that was only vaguely anticipated, and that has resulted in private ownership claims to portions of the human genome.

Let's look carefully at the history of the HGP and the emergence of human gene patents before considering some of the ethical implications posed by this new trend.

The Current Conundrum

The human genome has been mapped, and daily more of its territory becomes known and understood. The current map of the human genome is general, giving us a high-level view of the landscape, but much of it remains virgin territory. We have yet to understand precisely how the expression of the data represented by the map helps make us who we are and function as we do. Even so, the outlines of the territories of the map are being claimed, with nearly a fifth of the genome now staked out by various parties, patented against the claims of other newcomers.[1] In fact, the ability to stake those claims was largely responsible for the early completion of the HGP, spurred on by market competitors, and funded by the future value of ownership of DNA sequences and the pharmaceutical promise they hold.[2] While Craig Venter's company, Celera Corp., was investing millions in developing new rapid sequencing technologies, part of its value statement and justification to its shareholders for the tremendous capital outlays was the proposition that genes discovered in the process could be patented and become part of Celera's general portfolio of patents. As the US Patent and Trademark Office (PTO) began granting gene patents, other companies, individuals and institutions got into the act. Only after the fact did philosophers, lawyers, and activists begin to consider the practical, legal, and ethical implications of gene patents.

Numerous authors have since considered the practical and ethical issues involved in granting ownership over parts of the human genome. The range of considerations has spanned concerns over autonomy, dignity, economic efficiency, and other important ethical considerations. Most people, when confronted with the fact that their genetic code is now partly owned by a plethora of universities, corporations, and research institutes, visibly blanche and insist that it ought not to be so. It assuredly is so, and a quick search of the PTO filings will reveal thousands of patents currently owned on portions of your genome and mine.[3] How can this be? Is it right? Don't you own your own genetic code or isn't it at least a commonly-owned human good? These questions have been posed, and various ethicists, legislators, lawyers, and theologians have answered in differing ways. Some attempts have been made to reconcile these varied points of view into declarations, codes, and even laws meant to either settle the ownership question, to create means of remuneration, or to prevent ownership of the human genome or its parts. For instance, in 2000 the PTO, concerned about "patent stacking" by which companies were filing patents on genes with no yet-known utility, imposed more stringent requirements for utility claims in gene patent applications. As well, some lawmakers have attempted to stop the patenting of gene altogether, as with Congressmembers' Becerra and Weldon's H.R. 977, "The Genomic Research and Accessibility Act," which has not yet passed. Still, thousands of new patents continue to issue every year, and the public domain in the human genome continues to shrink.[4]

I have written in the past about the nature of intellectual property in general, arguing that there is no natural possessory right to *expressions* (man-made objects, intentionally produced),[5] and that we are free to create laws regarding the ownership of expressions as we see fit. I have argued that the dichotomy that pitches "utilitarian" versus "aesthetic" expressions, inherent in the distinct realms of copyright and patent, is confusing and ontologically unsound. In truth, expressions are all of a kind, falling along a spectrum, but in no sense are the natural categories of patent and copyright law mutually exclusive. I have argued that understanding the errors of the current ontology (our understanding of the nature of the objects themselves and their relations to each other) of intellectual property leaves us free to restructure our systems of ownership of expressions in more sensible and efficient ways to carry out better the goals of the authors of Article 1, Section 8 of the US Constitution. Given that intellectual property law is the currently accepted and yet most troubling context for discussing whether one ought to be able to exert property rights over the human genome or its parts, it is natural for me to begin with the methodology I have used in the past, namely: exploring the underlying ontological issues and assumptions and considering whether these have a sound basis, or whether we need a fresh perspective.

My methodology rests on a few general assumptions which I believe are uncontroversial, and while much of what follows depends in part on those assumptions, other elements of my argument are merely pragmatic, resting on no particular methodology. To be fair, I assume the following: 1 that while genes do not fully determine who we are, they are largely responsible for our individual traits, 2 that while we can never know anything with absolute certainty, science works because it accepts as true certain foundational beliefs, and 3 that *justice* is real, not merely invented by human preferences, but founded upon certain immutable, inherent natural kinds. For the philosophers reading this, this makes me more or less a genetic essentialist, a foundationalist, and a natural law theorist, if we must use labels. Nonetheless, while these assumptions work behind much of my argument, other less philosophical, and more clearly pragmatic arguments discussed later lead to many of the same conclusions about gene patenting. Moreover, the arguments made by others who have addressed this issue also hinge upon various philosophical assumptions, and they have ranged over a variety of common themes. Whatever their underlying assumptions, the literature and ongoing debate regarding the ethics of genome ownership has so far centered on discussing the following issues:

1   Is the generic human genome part of some collective human heritage?
2   Can individuals exert property rights over their individual genomes?
3   Do patents and other forms of intellectual property protection fairly produce economic efficiencies and innovation?
4   Can states or communities justly regulate economic exploitation of populations' genomes collected in databases?

All of these issues are important and worth considering, and viewpoints differ markedly. However, no one has adequately addressed a much more basic question which would frame each of these debates, namely: what are the relations among the following entities: individuals, populations, species, the generic "human genome," and the specific genome of an individual?

In other words, we need to work out the ontology of the above-named entities to better frame the context for the ethical debates about rights, genes, and property. Although there is clearly an inherent or assumed ontology underlying the present debate, our intuitions suggest that it is ill-conceived and worth reconsidering before we draw conclusions. For instance, the current legal and social framework for ownership rights presently being granted and recognized by patents seems at first glance to be unsound, and various attempts to clarify, restrain, or contain that framework have failed for one reason or another. Let's look at the science in light of the current framework and those attempts to re-conceive it, and ask whether all of these efforts have jumped the gun and made erroneous ontological assumptions.

The Objects of Our Study

Except for some viruses that rely only on RNA, all living things are built by the interaction of DNA and RNA within cells and their environments. Deoxyribonucleic acid (DNA) was discovered well before its central function in reproduction, cell differentiation, development, and ongoing existence of organisms was fully realized. It consists of four bases, – thymine, guanine, cytosine, and adenine, – held together by a phosphate "backbone" and famously revealed by Watson and Crick to twist in a double helix. Because thymine always pairs with adenine and cytosine always pairs with guanine, replicating the three billion base pair length of a full human genome requires only enzymatic splitting of that DNA. In other words, when you split it in half down its length, two complete copies of the strand can form due to the natural pairing of the bases. Although part of a highly complex process, the simplicity and necessity of the structure of DNA as revealed through the work of Watson, Crick, Wilkins, and Franklin, is immediately apparent. DNA is the code upon which the physical machine of an individual is built, and upon which it builds its offspring. All of the mechanical functioning of the organism is bound up with this molecule in conjunction with scores of other ongoing cellular and biological processes and the environment, all nonetheless wholly dependent for their inception and continuation on that code.

Reproduction of all organisms involves the reproduction of the code of an organism's DNA to produce a new organism. In the case of parthenogenesis – the way amoebas reproduce, by splitting themselves in two – the organism's exact code is merely duplicated (although mutations inevitably occur over generations). In the case of sexual reproduction, the codes of two organisms are recombined into a new, unique individual. While biologists had noted that certain traits appear to be inherited by offspring with predictable frequencies, the mechanism of that inheritance was not fully understood until the role of DNA was revealed. The "genes" responsible for certain traits are instructions embedded within an entire DNA sequence to turn on and off the production of various proteins at various stages of development or function. The entire sequence, all three billion base pairs, for an individual, exists in each cell of an organism. As cells differentiate, however, certain parts of the genome necessary for the proper function of discrete organs remain switched "on" while others are switched "off" according to the organ or system in which that cell is situated. DNA is organized into triplets or "codons" each of which is responsible for the production of a known protein, and which by working together constitute genes of various lengths. Codons are the syntax for the language of DNA.[6]

DNA directs protein production and metabolism indirectly by interacting with messenger RNA, ribosomes, and other organelles (see Chapter 3 for more discussion of these parts of cells) in each cell. The nucleus, where the DNA is harbored, is essentially a central processing unit that mediates cellular and biological development and function for an entire organism, and it transmits the evolutionary adaptations of the species from one generation to the next. In the sense that an entire species shares much of the same genome, the generic genome of a species is a unique entity, distinct from each instance of that genome in the form of individual members of the species. The genome of the species defines the general characteristics of a species, and the unique genome of an individual defines the unique characteristics of an individual. Thus the "human genome" is an abstracted entity, characterizing in general the human species, consisting of certain necessary collections of genes.

The "code" analogy is helpful, as indeed we are learning to decipher the instructions that compose the nearly 25,000 human genes, and to understand how they relate to the development of individuals of a species, and to the evolution of a species itself. This code, however, is unlike most manmade codes in that it underlies the formation of the second critical object of our study, namely – *persons*. We are only interested in the moral consequences of owning portions of the human genome because it impacts persons, and persons are the typical objects of moral consideration. Human beings and persons are distinct social entities. Human beings can be dead, or lack consciousness or the capacity for consciousness, but persons cannot. Persons are conscious or potentially conscious, rights-bearing, and duty-bound creatures.

So, critical to our study will be uncovering the relationships among DNA, genes, the "human genome," human beings, and persons. At some level, the higher level social objects we call *persons* consist of the interaction of the DNA molecule with a body, mind, and the environment. All of the higher-level functions that we associate with personhood depend ontologically on the chemical processes forming a person's day-to-day development and functioning. Before we make decisions about the justice of allowing ownership of parts of the human genome, we ought to attempt to describe those relations in order to discern whether property relations among those entities are proper or even conceivable.

The Legal Framework So Far

In the western world, the law of intellectual property has prescribed the legal bounds for ownership of genes and other portions of the genome. There are a number of reasons for this, including two important legal decisions, *Chakrabarty* and *Moore*.[7]

Chakrabarty established the principle allowing for patents on genetically engineered organisms, and *Moore* established that individuals do not have ownership rights over the fruits of discoveries made by harvesting of their DNA.[8] Between these two cases, and a massive land-grab for parts of the human genome initiated by Celera Corp.'s entry into the HGP race, the borders of the current situation were drawn by the PTO, courts, and corporations without much in the way of public involvement or ethical consideration, much less any sound ontological investigation. Despite the fiat boundaries set by these forces, there is no public consensus over the justice of the status quo.

Most ordinary people do not seem viscerally to accept the fact that products of nature, tied up with all human DNA, could be declared to be private property. Moreover, no other analogous legal entity enjoys this status. Partly because DNA is "unique," as argued by those who promote "genetic exceptionalism," the current state of affairs goes largely unchallenged in the public sphere, despite considerable philosophical and practical objections.

The arguments are plentiful and strong in favor of exceptionalism, though some reasoned objections to the notion have been made.[9] DNA is indeed unique, but there is very little in-depth argument tying together DNA's clear uniqueness and its current legal and social status. In order to do that work, more must be done than simply highlighting DNA's uniqueness. What are the relationships among DNA, identity, personhood, rights, duties, and property? Are there any analogous objects that might inform these issues?

A number of conflicting statements from world leaders and international organizations have challenged the current framework, suggesting that DNA may be part of a "common human heritage" and thus not prone to private ownership, or suggesting that individuals themselves own the rights to their own DNA. These alternative frameworks have been proposed late in the game, and rarely adopted, to little net effect in the race to patent portions of the human genome.[10]

The stakes under the current framework are significant and should be cause for concern. Objections to patenting genes are not alarmist nor simply academic. Besides the obvious impact on justice, the practical consequences of patenting segments of DNA without ethical clarity about the subject may include increased litigation, costlier research and therapies, and the potential for significant and costly conflicts regarding unintentional infringements. The economic incentives of patent are also significant, and if the current framework can be sorted out in order to dampen controversies regarding the practice, then important research can flourish without unnecessary impediment. Currently, and without adequate reason, DNA is being treated like software, steam engines, man-made chemical compounds, and other more likely candidates for patent. It is not yet too late to consider whether there is a sound theoretical basis for this.

We can challenge DNA patents on a number of grounds, including ethical objections to owning life or living tissues, or upon notions of human dignity. We might also challenge the economics and practicality of gene patents which arguably interfere with scientific research and innovation. All of this discussion ought to follow some more basic inquiry into the nature of DNA and genes themselves, and whether they properly fit into any existing paradigms of ownership or property. These categories inform our moral choices, and consist of a number of basic possibilities. DNA and genes might be property like other forms of property, like hammers, cars, or homes. Or possibly genes are properly considered to be intellectual property, sharing all essential qualities with other forms of intellectual property. Finally, genes and DNA might be a form of commons, immune to ordinary forms of possession or ownership. Let's briefly look at each of these paradigms.

The Property Paradigm

Property is perhaps one of the oldest concepts in law, and it is not surprising that it has arisen as a dominant theme in arguments for control over DNA. The most common forms of property historically include: real property (land), moveables (hammers, cars, etc.), and chattels (cattle, goats, etc.). Each of these forms of property can arguably arise extra-legally, with the brute facts of ownership exerted by possessors and those who literally stake out the bounds of their possessory interests. Possession is extralegal in that it is a fact independent of any legal or social facts. It is a brute fact as described by Searle's account of social reality, the brute facts of the world exist with or without human intentions. The legal and social status of *ownership* follows the brute facts of possession.[11]

The Intellectual Property Paradigm

As I have argued in *The Ontology of Cyberspace*, there is no "natural" or brute fact possession of the expressions (the "types" or universals at least) we have chosen to protect via intellectual property law. If we can say that certain forms of natural possessory facts are legally valid or validated by the legal institutions of property and ownership, we cannot say anything similar about intellectual property law. We are free, essentially, to create intellectual property laws as we wish, unbounded by concerns of justice and validity with respect to brute facts of possession. This is because there is no *natural* way to possess the "type" of an expression – anyone may easily copy most expressions without depriving the original author or creator of anything. Intellectual property law is an expedient designed to improve economic efficiency. Certain types of objects fit neatly into the categories we have created for intellectual property law, although the broad category of such objects is, as I have argued, simply "man-made objects intentionally produced." All intellectual property has, until recently, fallen easily into this broad category. The subcategories of copyright and patent have covered the spectrum of those man-made, intentionally produced objects whose uses have been primarily aesthetic (copyrightable) to those whose uses are primarily utilitarian (and thus patentable), but there is no natural basis by which to draw clear lines between these two ends of the spectrum of expressions. Thus, I have proposed a unitary scheme of intellectual property protection based upon the ontology of the entities involved and arguments for efficiency.[12]

Is the genome or are genes intellectual property? Are we similarly free to define the bounds of ownership and property rights over the human genome, or are there brute facts grounding certain valid claims and not others? Are genes or the genome even expressions of the sort which can have intellectual property protection under the current legal scheme?

The Commons Paradigm

There is no world-wide consensus yet as to whether portions of the human genome should be granted intellectual property protection, as indeed they are in the US and a number of other nations.[13] Some international agreements, conventions, and experts have argued that genetic exceptionalism requires we treat human DNA not as property to be owned by individuals nor granted intellectual property status, but rather as a common good. The notion of the commons involves goods which are difficult to contain, over which no natural, brute facts of ownership are easily exerted, and for which general public well-being argues against individual ownership. Examples of parts of the world typically agreed to be a part of the commons include: air, fresh water, airwaves, outer space, and airspace. These sorts of things cannot be enclosed, and treating these things as part of the commons enables the efficient working of markets by the fact of their common availability. Common goods may also not be appropriated by one without diminishing their value or amount to the community in general. Many have argued that ideas too are a part of the commons, and that intellectual property law unjustly encloses that which ought not to be enclosed.[14]

Various international and regional agreements as well as a handful of statutes have at one time or another described human DNA or the human genome as being part of a "common heritage" and thus uncloseable – in essence, a common good. Some notable features of common goods do seem to overlap with features of DNA, namely: it is not containable or enclosable to any natural exclusion of others, it is abundant and necessary for people in general to thrive, and it arguably benefits economic efficiency in some ways for it to not be circumscribed. On the other hand there are obvious differences between DNA and other common goods. For instance, each particular individual genome is theoretically unique to the individual, and can be appropriated with no diminution of its immediately useful value to the individual. The same may be argued about the generic "human genome." Its appropriation by one individual does not deprive humanity in general, and in fact may arguably enrich everyone given the health benefits expected to be achieved by scientific research and technological development conducted with the help of profits garnered through intellectual property protection. Still others have argued for creating a "contractual" commons for genetic information, purposely making policy decisions to share the resource, regardless of ontological claims about its status.[15]

We will consider these arguments in greater depth, after we explore first the proposed method for inquiry, and delve a bit more in-depth into the science which, I will argue, should first and foremost guide our decision-making.

Special Challenges of DNA

DNA is clearly unique. No other chemical or compound directs its own replication like DNA does. It has evolved a remarkable range of strategies for replication, resulting in all of the millions of species here on earth. Most of those species, in fact, share portions of their DNA with all the others. For instance, fruit flies and humans share genes that conduct similar processes and in all likelihood share the same historical evolutionary origin. Yet, genetic exceptionalism has not been reflected in any exceptional legal or social treatment.[16] Why, if DNA is so different than other types of compounds or objects, is it treated in the law as though it were just another man-made object, intentionally produced? Why are we shoving a double helix into a square hole? There may well be arguments to back this up, but they have not been well expressed. The most frequent arguments have been purely utilitarian, and the theoretical underpinnings are lacking.[17]

Ordinarily, products and laws of nature are not granted patent or other property protection. Yet today more and more human genes are claimed under various patents held by corporations and universities. These patents embody claims in most instances over the specific genetic sequences of the genes – the strings of base pairs that form the genes themselves, as well as techniques and processes associated with finding those specific strings. Patent protection has previously been limited only to inventions which are novel, useful, and new. Thus, if new naturally occurring compounds are discovered, no patent protection could ordinarily issue. There are a handful of exceptions to this general rule, the most notable being plant patents, but these have traditionally required some mixture of human innovation with a natural product to create something *new* and *useful*. Patents could be granted for *applications* of a new discovery to processes, or methods of synthesizing those compounds, but not for the structure of the compound itself. In the case of DNA, there is certainly a form of *legal* exceptionalism going on in the PTO. It is being treated now as a blatant exception to the general rule against patenting discoveries. Moreover, this exceptional legal treatment is being urged on the rest of the world through various international agreements and trade practices.

DNA poses numerous challenges to the current legal framework for protection, and may suggest developing an entirely new social and legal category recognizing its uniqueness. Ultimately, however, we should unravel the actual nature of the relations of DNA to individuals and species. We must delve into the ontology of the genome and its relationship to persons.

Property and Parts

As argued briefly above and in more depth in chapters to come, certain types of legal ownership are reflections of brute facts regarding possession that make such legally recognized rights and duties *grounded*. From this natural law perspective, just laws derive their justice from natural states of affairs. Positive legal theorists reject this notion, and argue that law and justice are purely human constructions with no particular grounding. According to positive legal theorists, we could simply legislate, for instance, that private property is unjust and should be illegal, make it a crime to own anything, and thus dispossess people of their property without moral or ethical repercussion.

I will argue in more depth later that the term "justice" fails to have any meaning under such a view, and state simply now that my argument is founded upon a modified natural law theory, in which there are such things as right and wrong, and just laws must be grounded in natural facts. Under this view, *justice* reflects an accurate correlation of laws and natural states of affairs. Thus, legal codes that recognize theft as conferring property rights are unjust. Socially and historically speaking, the sorts of things that can be owned legally are those whose possession can be asserted openly, publicly and maintained through various social acts. Those sorts of things that cannot be stolen or adversely occupied are generally treated as commons which cannot be owned by any one individual, but which must be shared by all. An in-depth analysis of property and property relations ought to precede determining that DNA can be property. Along the way, we will have to consider whether DNA is more like intellectual property, under which protection for genes is currently granted, or more like other forms of property. We may in fact discover that DNA is a unique type of object fit for unique property protection, or perhaps none at all.

We may also determine that DNA is not a distinct entity, but rather a part of another entity. This is an important distinction because the law does not generally recognize traditional property rights in one's own body parts, at least not of the sort encompassed by ordinary property claims. We might inquire into the justice of this prohibition, but it seems to be a rather universally accepted norm that one cannot alienate one's own body parts at whim. Is there a sound ontological basis for treating body parts this way? If so, is DNA to be treated like a body part?

In determining the relations of DNA to individuals, we will need to discern the mereology (the study of parts and boundaries) and topologies of highly complex objects. We won't complete that task in these pages, but we will certainly begin the task, pointing out important boundaries and features where we can. In so doing, we will need to elaborate the nature not just of the DNA that instructs the formation of a person, but of a person itself. One reasonable conclusion of our investigation may be that DNA and persons are holistic objects, incapable of reductionism. Such a conclusion could have significant implications for how we ought to treat DNA legally and socially.

There are many things in the world that never receive protection under property or intellectual property regimes. Not everything may be possessed, and there are legal restrictions on ownership of certain things.[18] It may well be that DNA fits under no current legal, cultural, or social scheme of ownership, and that genes are not the sorts of things that can be owned. Moreover, we might wish to clarify whether and to what extent our possession of our own individual genes extends to some sort of *rights* over those genes (both tokens and types). Not every act of possession confers a right, after all. Fully answering questions over the patentability of genes, or other ownership or possessory rights over them, will also rely upon a sound understanding of the relations between genes and ourselves as autonomous individuals.

Autonomy, Individuality, and Personhood

Many of our instincts about patenting DNA, and suspicions about its similarities to other more onerous forms of ownership of persons, may derive from our misunderstandings about the relationship of DNA to individuals and species. In this age of genetic reductionism, and of popular movies and books depicting cloning and genetic engineering, there is a rather frequent tendency to conflate our genes with *ourselves*. If indeed we are nothing but the products of our genes, then surely allowing others to own those genes is a form of slavery or something akin to it. This same tendency may also cause us to mistake the use of a particular population's genetic homogeneity with either racism or some form of unwarranted exploitation. While we may wish to make arguments about the justice of rewarding individuals who donate their tissues to science with remuneration more fitting than we have in the past (for instance, linked to profits, or with more balanced tangible benefits) we ought not to mistake genes for ethnic destiny. Neither should we make the reverse mistake and link historical accident with desert.

None of us is fully the product of our genes, as we shall see in subsequent chapters. Nor is any population, despite its relative genetic homogeneity, the architect of its genetic makeup – its nature is not the result of the sort of intention ordinarily required for invention. Our genetic diversity is greater than scientists previously suspected, even while the genes we share are shared widely and rather fully. That is to say, while you and I share 99 percent of our genes, the important stuff is going on in that 1 percent of difference. The differences amount to much more than genes as well. Information is encoded in the gaps between genes, single-nucleotide polymorphisms(SNPs), and copy number variations (CNV), all of which will be explained in more detail later. Suffice it to say for now, however, that you are not your genes and your genes are not you.

Genetic determinism is being challenged not just for philosophical reasons and without reference to any troubling intellectual puzzles like "free will." Rather, we are learning that the environment interacts with genes in complex ways over time. Epigenetics is the study of the relations and interactions among genes and their environments, and it is showing that genetic determinism or reductionism does not even work at the cellular level. There is reason to suspect that at a higher level, at the level of consciousness and personhood, the extent to which your genes determine who you are, or make you be you, has been exaggerated significantly.

We must account for all of this in deciding whether patenting genes violates more than mere legal norms, but also social or cultural traditions respecting notions of privacy and autonomy. We will thus delve into the relations of genes to autonomy, privacy, and some tricky concepts like *personhood* as we investigate the ethics of gene ownership in general. We'll have to look both at the science of individuality at the genetic level, and touch upon the nature of autonomy and personhood as they relate to our individual genetic make-ups.

All of these inquiries are nonetheless part of a recent context in which gene patents already abound. While justice demands we challenge the status quo, and perhaps even change it, we must also be mindful of the economic purposes of intellectual property law, and the likely impact of altering the present regime.

Economics and the Marketplace for Genes

Injustice alone may not be reason enough to significantly alter law or custom where the economic consequences of such a change would be too great. We should weigh the effects of the current situation against the likely effects of changing it. Clearly, there are numerous parties interested in maintaining the present system as they gain profits and are often motivated in part or wholly by the potential for economic reward. We should consider these motivations, the strength of other potential motivations, and other possible models that might accomplish the twin goals of scientific advance and profit within the confines of *justice*.

History is full of examples of the complex interactions among science, technology, and the marketplace. Scientific advance has long fueled technological progress and people have profited from both endeavors individually and collectively. The last century saw the development of new modes of scientific inquiry including so-called "big science" involving massive public investments in such things as the Manhattan Project, the space race, and particle physics. Scientific problems and technological solutions have benefited by the interaction of researchers, governments, and corporations in uncovering and exploiting natural phenomena. Some of those benefits have been economic. Science and technology now account for a large share of the world's fastest growing economies, and the public benefits along with researchers and technologists.

Overhauling the present system, even were it unjust, may not be warranted if economic upheaval would be the only result. It is difficult to justify massive deprivations of property rights, although it has been done before where injustice outweighed all other considerations. That may be the case with gene patents, but if it is not, then we should consider alternatives. It may also be that the deprivation of rights to gene patents need not ultimately alter much at all. It could well be that other means of protecting innovation currently exist, and that the patent system can be used more properly to protect innovation, perhaps in partnership with corporations and governments, and that economies could benefit from more clearly defining those rights and relationships.

Have science and technology worked in synchrony before in ways that are being ignored or even undermined with the development of gene patents? Is the *status quo* a perversion of how the marketplace and scientific discoveries have typically benefited each other? If so, can we normalize this relationship without collapsing a burgeoning marketplace? Might we even provoke greater investment and encourage faster discovery and invention by subtle changes to the ways we interpret the existing patent laws? We will look at all of these possibilities and consider the practical effects both politically and economically.

Ethics and Method

So far, those who have considered the issues raised above have done so by analogy, or by applying ethical theories of various sorts (such as consequentialism or Kantianism) to the present legal and social status of human DNA. This has been putting the cart before the horse. It assumes too much about the nature of DNA to accept its current *ontological* classification while arguing either for or against the ethics of its ownership. The best literature on the subject has argued for genetic exceptionalism, pointing out DNA's unique nature. Neither those who have done this good work, nor those who have prematurely argued either for or against the ethics of DNA ownership, have done the *foundational* work of describing the objective relations among genomes, genes, individuals, persons, and species. Only by first describing these relations can we begin to consider the justice of treating DNA as property, as a commons, or as something entirely new.

While I do not wish to argue from a particular ethical theory, neither consequentialism nor Kantianism, nor some other fixed ethical standpoint, my modified natural law standpoint assumes that there is such a thing as *justice*. Part of my argument will involve defending the claim that certain laws are *grounded* and others are not. If in fact there is no *justice*, and laws bear no relation to it, then there is no sense in evaluating the justice of any particular system or institution as against any other. I also assume that even those who call themselves consequentialists care about justice. Consequentialism concerns itself also with the "good" and is thus an ethical theory by which *justice* is often measured. There are many flaws more able philosophers have noted with both pure deontological (duty-based) and pure consequentialist theory. For instance, utility is itself based upon an arbitrary yet absolute value: happiness. Deontological theories of the good are flawed because they must admit of defeasible values, and evils must be weighed one against another. That is, when values conflict, common sense dictates that breaking some rules is worthwhile to defend other rules, like lying to prevent a murder. This undermines pure deontological ethics which says that moral rules may never be broken ethically.

These objections and arguments are well known. While the first stage of our investigation will seek to uncover the ontology of the genome in relation to persons, etc., we will at some point wish to make decisions about the *justice* of the present state of affairs as measured against other possible ways of dealing with DNA and genes in the law. In so doing we will look to bolster arguments I have mentioned so far in passing regarding the groundedness of certain legal institutions and objects, allowing for us to call certain of them "valid" and others not. We will also consider, for those not swayed by this particular definition of justice, the economic and practical utility of various schemes of treatment of human DNA.[19]

Ultimately, I will argue that our normative ethical decisions about property as an institution precede theory, and that pure ethical theories fail because they are not themselves scientific. They start from first principles rather than observation.[20] Institutions, laws, rules and customs are based, at some point, on brute facts. It is at that nexus, between pre-institutional or extralegal facts, and the institutions we devise, that *justice* as an ideal is either instituted or fails. Observation of brute facts, and careful examination of necessary relations that exist pre-institutionally, should pave the way for decisions about how or whether laws, customs, or social norms are supported by the natural conditions of the world.

An Outline for the Investigation

After some greater discussion of methodology, we will begin to look carefully at the science of the relations among the smallest constituent parts of our study, namely, the biochemistry of the genome. How are genes formed from their organic components, how do they interact with the environment, both at the cellular level and extra-cellularly, to produce proteins, and how do those proteins interact with the environment and each other to create a functioning unique organism? This inquiry will lead us to our first big philosophical puzzle: how does the mechanism described by these processes correlate to the social object we call a "person?" We will consider some problems of genetic determinism, including the role of genes in forming behaviors, and the role of the environment in interacting with genes and behaviors to shape the unique social continuants of, for instance, a Gandhi or a Hitler. The link between personhood and the genome is crucial to discerning whether DNA ought to be treated as property, part, or as some other object given that the social and legal institutions of property and ownership only apply to *persons.*

Next we will look into the relationships among individuals and species. DNA is not like any other known compound in that each individual's genome is unique, but all DNA shares certain general features. How are the general features of DNA reflected in the "human genome" as opposed to individual genomes? How are these similarities and differences reflected in individuals of a species versus the species itself? Uncovering these relations should help us discern the nature of individual or collective rights, if any, over the human genome or individual, unique genomes, or their parts.

We will examine the dimensions of gene ownership under current regulatory and legal regimes internationally. We will look also at cultural norms regarding ownership in general, and consider the application of various property and ownership norms to the special characteristics of the human genome and individuals' genomes. We will also look at the current dominant scheme of intellectual property protection for genes, consider to what degree genes are like other forms of intellectual property, and the degrees in which they differ. We will then compare this with objects that are generally considered to be part of the "commons" and analyze the ontology of common goods versus property in general before applying this to the special problem of the human genome. In what sense, if any, is the notion of a commons supported by the world of brute facts, and can an argument be made that the human genome is a part of that world?

In the process of considering the above, we will examine arguments in favor of moral realism based upon the "groundedness" of legal and social institutions. Examples from the relatively uncontroversial world of real property, moveables, and chattels will be compared with the human genome and individual genomes. We will also continue to discuss the relations between justice and groundedness under this particular version of moral realism and natural law theory.

Because we are concerned not just with pure theory, we will delve into practical considerations of both the current scheme of DNA protection and potential alternatives. What are the economic consequences of patent and other forms of protection? What results could we anticipate from treating DNA as a commons, and are there other possible means of achieving the goals of justice and spurring innovation by economic reward?

Finally, we will synthesize the results of the investigation to determine whether there is reason to accept the current situation, to modify it, or to revise it entirely. This holistic approach to the problem has not yet been conducted, and only by considering first the underlying ontological assumptions and applying them to existing and accepted norms of ownership and ethics may we reach considered opinions as to justice, which is our ultimate concern regarding DNA, the human genome, and patents.

The Challenge Ahead

Like it or not, we have plunged headlong into a world where large portions of the organic code that is responsible for the development and functioning of every living human being, and generations to come, is claimed as owned by various individuals, corporations, and institutions. These bits of code, in the forms of whole genes, expressed sequence tags (ESTs which indicate where certain genes are located) and even SNPs (which are unique changes in a single base pair), cannot be researched, manipulated, replicated, or innovated upon without infringing the ownership claims of the patent holders. There are real-world effects to this ownership, including undeniable effects on further development and research of the function and structure of the human genome. Groundbreaking pharmaceuticals, and greater understanding of the interactions between genes and health are coming to light every day as a result. Meanwhile, we are also experiencing increased litigation and costs associated with it. The complexity of the patent system, combined with the complexity of the genome, make inadvertent infringements and litigation inevitable.

If the current situation were ethically clear, then people would not react as they generally do when presented with the news that much of their genome is owned by someone. It is viscerally uncomfortable, and I suggest it is so because it conflicts with something we sense or know about the brute facts of our world and property relations that we tend to accept because they are grounded versus those that are ungrounded and unjust. Before we move further in the direction we are headed, we ought to sort out the relations among DNA, genes, human beings and persons, and consider how the present situation may or may not accommodate our sense of justice in according others rights over something upon which we all depend and to which we all owe the same debt for our existence.

2 | ETHICS AND ONTOLOGY
A BRIEF DISCOURSE ON
METHOD

Approaches to the Problem

Gene patenting began without public debate. It was enabled by strained interpretations of legal precedent, and with very little consideration of its ultimate ethical implications. The post hoc analysis has come in fits and starts and from a variety of ethical perspectives. As I have discussed above, other analyses focus on such things as utility, various pragmatic concerns, rights-based approaches, and theological ethics. The problem with this grab-bag of approaches is the problem of ethics as a field. How do we reach a consensus about ethical dilemmas posed by radical new technologies when philosophers have never succeeded in reaching consensus about ethical theories in general? Can we expect policy makers, much less the public, to make ethical decisions about complicated technological and scientific matters without a clear, universally acceptable ethical framework? It seems doubtful, and it should not be at all surprising that we find ourselves now in the midst of an untenable situation where fundamental questions remain unanswered.

If we are to make meaningful statements about what one *ought* to do and not do, and to judge certain actions, states of affairs, or even people as immoral or unethical, then we must try to find a standard by which such judgments can be made. The sciences of justice, ethics, and morals remain in their dark ages, with their practitioners all ascribing to differing values and modes of inquiry, besieged in their various camps of deontological, or consequentialist, or emotive, or theistic dogmas. What I propose is a methodological accord that serves to begin building a bridge among ethical investigators, and that grounds ethical studies in something objective by stepping back and inquiring first into the nature of the objects themselves – doing ontology.

The divergence of ethical schools rests upon differing notions of ultimate *value*. Very simply put, consequentialists regard "utility" as a fundamental value, Kantians regard "universalizability" and "duty" as ultimate values, emotivists consider "aesthetic feelings" as ultimate values. These values serve as measures by which those who ascribe to each ethical school distinguish between the "good" and the "not good." However, these values are ultimately quite arbitrarily chosen, and thus members of various ethical schools will never agree unless they can shift opponents over to their choice of values. This doesn't make for good science. While all of those who do ethical inquiry practice ontology by categorizing into "good" or "not good," they use differing measures to class the objects of their study.[1]

However, insight about the role of ontology in ethics might serve as a point of departure for conducting ethical inquiry that disregards differences in ultimate value and that could bridge these schools. Let's begin with the common ontological basis of all ethical investigation, and see how we might expand on it ecumenically. To do so, let's set aside "value" for the moment and look at the objects, acts, and intentional states of actors in themselves. Let's first ask first whether certain states of affairs are "grounded" and others not.

Groundedness as an Empirical Measure

For empiricism to succeed and for objective claims about justice to be meaningful, there must be certain underlying and objective facts that exist despite our judgments, but which might still serve as bases for making judgments. When we ask questions about the nature of "murder" or "theft," we can see that these are ultimately ontological issues. These categories require answering questions about the natures of "life" and "property" in certain contexts. To determine whether a particular killing is wrong, or what we more commonly refer to as a "murder," we first must make decisions about whether a person may take a life of another person under certain conditions. If the context is, for instance, a "war" and the two persons legal combatants, then our judgments about whether the killing is a murder are different than if the context is a traffic dispute during peacetime and the two persons are automobile drivers. No matter which ethical tradition we choose, or which standpoint we take, decisions about classifying types of action, such as killing under certain conditions, should be able to be agreed upon. These decisions can be as grounded as our knowledge about other more specific states of affairs.

When we say something is grounded, we mean it has an empirically verifiable basis in objective facts. Adolf Reinach, in his *Apriori Foundations of the Civil Law*,[2] describes this groundedness using examples from mathematics. The example he gives is that the sum of 2 and 2 is always 4. The truth of the statement "$2 + 2 = 4$" is empirically verifiable and thus grounded. Reinach moves to a discussion of the ontology of claims and obligations arising from the acts of promising and explains that claims are grounded in the facts of this ontology. Whenever a promise is made and accepted both through speech and someone's intention, then claims and duties arise as real things in the world, and the fact of the existence of claim is grounded as fully as the facts of mathematics. Without this groundedness, then, the acts and intentions of promising as a social act become meaningless. Under this ontology of the pre-legal institution of promising, the law of contract is grounded just as the facts of mathematics are. Consider a world where this is not the case. If the exchange of promises and consideration were not necessarily linked ontologically with the simultaneous creation of real claims and obligations, each of which disappear with the fulfillment of the agreement, then words like "I promise" or "I will owe" become mere poetry having no relation to anything real. But we use the terms and intentions associated with promising meaningfully, and thus the moral requirement to abide by promises is grounded in the facts of the social ontology of promising.

Consider a standard ethical question regarding the morality of theft. Various ethical schools may regard individual acts of theft differently, coming up with cases at the peripheries that challenge our moral intuitions about whether a particular theft (that is, the taking by one person of another person's property) may be morally acceptable. There is another ontological question at the heart of all questions about theft that ethicists of all stripes can resolve – namely, what is the ontology of property? What types of things under which conditions count as property? Before we can begin to delve into the ethics of theft, we need to uncover the *nature of property* in general, and ask whether and to what extent the institution of ownership is grounded in any of the simple and necessary facts regarding property just as Reinach did with claims and contracts.[3] None of this inquiry presupposes a standpoint from a particular ethical school. Rather, we must investigate the nature of things that can be possessed, under what conditions, and due to which intentional states and outward acts such things can be possessed and owned validly. I have argued, for instance, that ideas are not the sort of thing that can be naturally possessed. That is to say, while a particular token of an expression may be possessed, the type cannot be. In *The Ontology of Cyberspace*,[4] I make the case that the nature of ideas as fleeting, intangible, unbounded objects makes exclusive possession of them a ludicrous and impossible concept. While the token (for instance, the sheet music or recording) of a particular song may be possessed, the nature of the type makes it impossible to exclude others from its possession and duplication or reproduction. I conclude that intellectual property law is thus not grounded in any facts of nature, and thus legal regimes regarding such "property" are entirely positive (purely man-made), having no natural foundation.

What of tangible property? What is it about the possession of a token that differs from that of a type, and does this make property law concerning "moveables" grounded in a way intellectual property laws are not? How about land, otherwise called "real property"? A complete ontology of property, which should precede decisions about the ethics of theft, would uncover the necessary relations of persons to objects and to land, and even to other persons. I suspect that such an ontology would reveal that there are certain such relations that make the social and legal institutions of *ownership* grounded, and thus the ethics of theft more clear. If indeed some object is possessed in ways that properly exclude others' possession, then the deprivation of that possession would have the same moral status as the violation of a claim or obligation.[5]

A Case in Point

In these pages, I have concerned myself with the legal and moral treatment of ownership of human DNA. There are scores of scholarly articles and some books that consider the ethical dilemmas posed by gene ownership – particularly human gene ownership. Most make considered arguments from the viewpoint of some ethical school of thought, examining whether and how allowing human genes to be patented conflicts with core values of those schools, such as "utility" or "dignity." While a few of the scholarly works on this subject do argue that DNA is "exceptional," none probe the several fundamental ontological issues underlying this question regardless of ethical approach. All assume too much without sorting out first the nature of the objects involved in gene ownership.

How does DNA differ from other objects of ownership, if at all? If DNA is an object like expressions, then we can consider legal institutions that afford rights over their reproduction, and so on, to be as just like regimes that provide ownership over other forms of expressions (like intellectual property). Similarly, if DNA is a moveable (like a hammer or a car) then we can devise valid means of ownership over its possession and ownership just like we do for hammers and Hummers™. Many have inquired into whether DNA can be patented under present laws, or whether intellectual property rights over genes offend our ethical intuitions, but we can look at these questions from another perspective – one that seeks to understand first the nature of the objects themselves before making ethical judgments. What is DNA and how does it relate to other objects? How does human DNA differ from the DNA of other creatures? What sorts of creatures can own things and in what manners? What sorts of things can be owned and in what ways?

These may look like standard ethical questions, but a careful ontological analysis may be applied to these questions without ethical bias. What follows in these pages is an attempt to accomplish this analysis, considering the status first of each component object before delving into an ethical analysis. Each of these questions involves a careful study of the social ontology of ownership, personhood, and the institutions of science and property in general. These institutions have features which, like those of claims and promising, arise from human intentions combined with actions, and do so pre-legally. Certain states of affairs about these institutions may in fact be grounded, and others may not. As I mentioned above, ownership and property rights in moveables (tangible goods that are non-fungible, roughly, "non-exchangeable", see Chapter 4 for further discussion) are good candidates for grounded relations as opposed to intellectual property. In other words, my possession of an object excludes that of another person's quite naturally. The law reflects this relation in the old adage "possession is nine-tenths of the law." Thus, when we encounter a situation in which one person possesses something, there is both a legal and moral presumption that this person has come into its possession properly against all other claims to that property. Thus, taking the possession of another's already possessed object is considered prima facie wrong, and can only be supported by proof that the original possessor came to possess the object wrongly (for instance, by violence or by theft) in the first place.

Moveable objects may be possessed in a number of ways: originally (as an object originally found or made by the possessor), as part of a transfer (something was exchanged by the current possessor for the object), by "finder's keepers" (where the original owner has carelessly misplaced the object, and the object has been found by the new possessor), as a gift (where the original possessor gave the object to the new possessor without any exchange or expectation of recompense), or by a "taking" (where the new possessor has taken an object possessed by another without any exchange). This list exhausts the conditions under which moveables may come to be possessed, but what about the ethical status of these various modes of possession? In fact, we recognize all but the last situation as valid modes of possession, which the law calls "ownership." I would argue that only the final mode of possession is not "grounded" and this is why we consider it to be "theft" under the law, and morally and ethically wrong under almost every ethical mode of inquiry.

The Groundedness of Ownership of Moveables

The groundedness of a valid possession rests on the intentional state of the possessor and other external and objective facts of the possession. An original possessor comes into the possession intending to possess the object and without having any knowledge of another's prior claim, nor with any intent to deprive another of a prior claim. The finder of a lost object holds the same intent. In both of these contexts, there are no indicia of ownership by another, and thus the intent not to deprive another is genuine and remains valid against all other claims of prior possession. If moveables could always be held and carried around everywhere, then claims of prior possession would all be easy to discern. One's exclusive possession of an object is prima facie evidence of valid possession, and an attempt to take an object from a possessor in current possession is an invasion, easy to discern, and plainly wrong. The law calls this robbery. Because moveables may not always be in one's present possession, other indicia of ownership are generally necessary to defeat claims of possession by others. These indicia include: marking the object in some way (with one's name, for instance), or keeping the object in an area delineated as one's own (in one's home, locker, desk, etc.). Indicia of prior possession give notice to those who might come into an object's possession that the object is already claimed as another's and thus anyone else's attempt at possession is intended to deprive the first of a valid claim of ownership. New attempts at adverse possessions cannot have a valid intent and are thus improper, ungrounded "takings" even though the current possessor might not be in actual present possession. The law calls this burglary or theft, and again, it is plainly wrong under most ethical theories.[6]

Valid transfers such as exchanges (for instance, by barter or purchase) and gifts involve parties who intend not to deprive another of a present possession or claims of possession, but rather to confer possession from one proper possessor to another. In the case of an exchange, something of mutually agreed value is given by a proper possessor of that thing (or fungible item such as money) and the object is transferred in consideration of that exchange. Two simultaneous exchanges thus take place and each actor in the exchange intends to confer possession to the other. In the case of a gift, transfer of possession is intended without any expectation of consideration or recompense.

The ontology of the social and legal institution of *ownership* reveals that it is grounded in certain states of affairs, such as brute-worldly facts and intentional states, as well as social acts revealing intentions of the parties. These states of affairs are pre-legal, and positive codes that might seek to alter the validity of ownership in general (e.g., by arguing that *all* property is theft), or to invalidate certain types or conditions of ownership shown to be valid above, would not themselves be grounded. Of course, so far we cannot make the case that all laws, ethics, or morals *must* be grounded. It is *conceivable* that we would enact a law or ethical precept that 2 + 2 actually should equal 5 and will hereafter. I suspect we all have similar repulsions against this Orwellian possibility. I'm pretty certain that we would even argue that such regimes are unjust.

So Where Does Ontology Get Us?

Here's what we can say so far: ethics, inasmuch as it involves the classification of certain states of affairs, intentional states, values, and actions as either wrong or right, is itself a subfield of ontology. But more importantly, many ethical questions are attacked prematurely, without regard for fundamental ontological issues assumed too quickly, such as discerning the nature of persons, property, or even rights (which we haven't even touched on here). I would argue that were we to step back from the biases of various ethical schools of thought, and first attack the basic problems of *what certain things are and how they relate to other things*, we would start to reveal why it is that we classify certain things as wrong or right. As discussed so cursorily above, the legal and moral institutions of ownership, theft, etc., all depend upon certain pre-legal, pre-ethical states of affairs including intentional states, brute facts, and social acts. It is not an accident that the law of property has embodied this ontology, and that nearly every ethical school of thought regards certain claims of possession as invalid (as thefts, for instance) and others as valid. I believe this method of inquiry avoids what philosophers call the "naturalistic fallacy," which is the fallacy of attempting to define the good by reference to "natural" properties such as desirability or happiness. This is part and parcel of the objections I make above to the arbitrary grounding of ethical values. G. E. Moore's description of the fallacy is correct, but the method I propose looks first to the *things in themselves* without regard to the "good" at all. For instance, the justice of property law has nothing to do with happiness. It derives from the facts of possession and the relations between persons and objects. We must first define the objects, then the nature of "the good" becomes clear.

Finally, the application of ontology, by which we seek to understand the nature of objects (broadly construed, since persons are objects) and their relations to one another, may reveal a new direction for ethical inquiry itself based upon the notion of *groundedness*. Of course, it could be argued that by doing so we have replaced one alleged fundamental value with another in that groundedness of legal, moral, or ethical concepts simply replaces utility or universalizability. Maybe so, but groundedness has the advantage of being empirically observed, through thorough ontological analysis of observable states of affairs. Intentional states exist, as do brute facts such as possession. Social facts can be observed in acts such as promising or gifting. Finally, legal institutions, which have been long-standing expressions of notions of right or wrong, seem often to coincide with groundedness of ethical and moral precepts. Thus, careful analysis of the ontology of existing institutions helps us to unravel the nature of pre-legal states of affairs and aids our judgment of ontological groundedness of moral claims.

In the case, for instance, of the ethics or morality of claims of ownership of human DNA by patent, ontology gives us a starting point that seems unbiased. Some initial questions are obvious: what is DNA really, and how does it relate to persons? Is DNA the sort of thing over which property claims are properly grounded? Is it a moveable, chattel, real estate? Is it a commons? Is the current treatment of DNA as intellectual property consistent with its nature? Ethics seems to not only be a subfield of ontology, as argued above, but impossible to pursue rationally without a thorough ontological analysis of all its objects. This is what we'll do next, by beginning to look carefully at the objects involved, sorting out their relations to each other, and then investigating whether and how natural states of affairs might inform the ethical status of gene patents. We'll begin first with the science, and see where that leads us.

3 | THE SCIENCE
GENES AND PHENOTYPES

It is clichéd, but it is fact: deoxyriboneucleic acid (DNA) is the chemical basis for all life on earth. It is a complex, long, polymer-like compound, composed of four amino acids: adenine, guanine, cytosine, and thymine. These four amino acids bond along a phosphate backbone in the now familiar structure of the double helix. Every thymine bonds across the "rung" in the spiral ladder with an adenine, and every cytosine with a guanine. Thus, by breaking the rung, and splitting the long strand of an organism's DNA, a perfect copy of the organism's original DNA can be made. When organisms reproduce asexually, perfect copies of their DNA are in fact made, and the resulting offspring are essentially clones of the original. Simple organisms, like bacteria, do just this. Organisms that reproduce sexually combine the DNA of each parent to form offspring with unique DNA which differs from each parent. Offspring from sexual reproduction nonetheless tend to share various traits with their parents, which was the clue to the genetic theory in the first place. Long before DNA was known to exist, and before it was known that it had something to do with our behaviors, diseases, and appearances, genetics was used in the selective breeding of agricultural products, including grains, vegetables, and livestock. It was not until the twentieth century that DNA was recognized as the fundamental mechanism for passing on traits from parents to offspring.

Before we look at the relations of traits (which include many behaviors, and a good deal of what we can assume for now make us who we are as *persons*) to DNA and its functioning, we'll recount briefly its discovery and trace the development of scientific knowledge about DNA to date. This will help non-specialists understand its role in biology, and help us to begin understanding an ontology of DNA, genes, and metabolism. Ultimately, we will need to find the links between those rudimentary but fundamental entities as well as *individuals*, and the much higher-level social object we call *persons*. We cannot complete this task here, but we can certainly define its boundaries, note its importance, and make an initial foray into this vital territory.

Understanding the nature of genes and DNA is also part of an argument I'll make below about the role of individuals in directing the use of their personal DNA. As new technologies emerge that allow us to know more about our individual genetic makeup, and as more of our personal genetic information becomes publicly available, or available to private for-profit concerns, it behooves us to learn more about the science. A more educated public and smarter individuals will hopefully become better stewards of their own genetic information and make wiser choices about it. We must also understand the science to make better legal choices about how to treat it, either in legislation, or by contract. DNA sampling is now included in many clinical medical trials, whether they are DNA studies or not. These samples then become part of either private or public repositories, known as bio-banks, which may be drawn upon at any time in the future for research or even mined for potential profits. Understanding the nature and science of DNA will help us make better choices about participating in clinical trials, and agreeing to the use of our genetic resources. As I will argue in future chapters, it may also help ensure our privacy if we decide to call for legislation that grants new privacy rights to our personal genetic information. A quick look at the science and its historical development is therefore a good place to start.

Classical Genetics

Since at least as far back as Aristotle (*Generation of Animals*, Book 4), observers of domesticated animals and human families have noted that traits tend to be passed from one generation to the next. Aristotle proposed that these traits were inherent in the blood, and the blood of the parents would be expressed in the traits of the children. This notion of inheritance involved a "mixing" of traits, on a more or less 50/50 basis. The notion of "blended" inheritance in this manner stuck until the mid nineteenth century. Even Charles Darwin held a similar view of the nature of how traits evolved and were passed on. It took a now-famous monk, obsessed with peas, to unravel a more accurate description of simple inheritance.

The notion of "genetic" inheritance, or "particular" inheritance, with certain traits passed on through individual genes, was first devised by Gregor Mendel in 1865. Particular inheritance explains, for instance, how the child of a blue-eyed, blonde-haired mother, and a brown-haired, brown-eyed father, can end up with blue eyes and brown hair. Traits are not passed on by the blending of traits (say a dirty-blonde, hazel-eyed offspring) but rather by the passing on of certain genes, which may or may not be "dominant" over other genes, to create unique offspring with a mathematically determinable incidence of traits.[1]

Mendel conducted his experiments on inheritance (not yet coined "genetic") using pea plants (*pisum sativum*) which just so happened to have single-gene traits. This was a lucky accident, because most plants and animals have a variety of traits that turn out to be determined by more than one gene at a time, which only complicates the mathematical analysis. But the pea plant was ideal and available. He distinguished peas by their color (green or yellow), their skin texture (either smooth or wrinkled), flower type (either axial or terminal . . . with flowers along the axis of the stem, or at the end of individual stems), and stem type (long or short). Once again, and fortunately for his analysis and contribution to an early understanding of genetic inheritance, these traits are each determined by single genes (soon to be defined). Mendel carefully interbred plants with each of these various traits, pollinating them painstakingly by hand and noting the development of each resulting generation of offspring. Mendel discovered early on in his studies that certain traits or "characters" were "pure" in that they showed no variation so that each generation, when either self- or cross-pollinated, produced offspring with the same character. He established lines that bred "true" for each of the character traits, or *phenotypes* (which literally means "the form is shown") which he would study. He then carefully interbred these lines and noted the ratios of characters of resulting offspring.

The first critical fact he noted was that pure lines did not result in mixed offspring. Purple-flowered plants, no matter with what other type of plant they crossed, always resulted in purple offspring in the next generation. This suggested the "blended" notion of inheritance was wrong.[2] The next stage of his studies proved to be the beginning of modern genetic studies. He carefully interbred and cross-bred various lines and counted the occurrence of resulting phenotypes. He noted that, for instance, round peas crossed with wrinkled ones resulted in the first generation of self-pollinated offspring in a generation of all-round seeds, whereas in the second generation of self-pollination, the wrinkled trait reappeared in 1,850 out of 7,324 plants.[3] The ratio of smooth to wrinkled was 2.96 to 1. He found, with six traits in all, that the same ratio of roughly 3 to 1 kept appearing, with the disappearance of one parental trait in the first self-pollinated generation, and reappearing in the second generation in a quarter of the offspring. Mendel used the terms "dominant" and "recessive" to classify the traits, noting that, for instance, a purple-flowered plant maintains the *potential* or recessive character of a white-flowered parent.[4]

Before genes were proposed or discovered to be the medium for inheritance of these traits, Mendel had determined through empirical means the fact and statistical truths of such inheritance. Eventually, observations of dyed chromosomes enabled scientists to roughly observe and track gene pairs which helped lead to the hypothesis that the stuff that composes chromosomes, namely DNA, was the medium for genes and thus genetic inheritance. Mendel continued his observations of multiple traits and incidence of inheritance, leading to a further conclusion that, in general, traits are essentially uncoupled from one another (later shown not to be entirely true as traits near one another on the same chromosome do often travel together). These are significant insights, brought about by Mendel's careful study, and only later recognized for their true importance. Although breeders of plants and domesticated animals had for centuries employed these principles, the mechanism was only fully appreciated in the early twentieth century. In the mid twentieth century, scientists began to unravel the complex structure of DNA, and once that structure was fully appreciated, it became clear that it was the primary mechanism for inheritance, evolution, and all the development and metabolism of every independent living creature.

Modern Genetics

In the early twentieth century, as microscopy began to reveal in detail the processes of cell *mitosis* and *meiosis*, chromosomes emerged as the most likely carriers of *genes*. By observing cellular division, the processes by which cells replicate either in somatic cells[5] (mitosis) or in gametes (meiosis), scientists observed bodies that behaved in interesting ways. Specifically, these chromosomes (literally, colored bodies) were present in identical numbers in every cell of an organism's body, and that number was the same in every member of the same species. By observing the processes of cellular division, it became apparent that the nuclear bodies, which organized themselves into these observable chromosomes during replication, might well be the carriers of genetic material responsible for observable phenotypes. In 1902, two researchers working independently formulated the chromosomal theory of genetic inheritance. Their names were Walter Sutton and Theodor Boveri. By dyeing and observing chromosomes, they confirmed that Mendelian inheritance patterns were correlated with chromosomal indicators. It is the process of meiosis that causes the combination and expression of genetic traits in unique offspring, where dominant and recessive traits follow the inheritance of some sort of data in the chromosomes (not yet known to be DNA), that becomes expressed somehow in the offspring. In 1913, Elinor Carothers helped confirm the theory in a species of grasshopper. In 1909, Thomas Hunt Morgan helped to explain so-called sex-linkage of traits, by which certain traits follow the chromosomes responsible for the gender of the offspring, further confirming the chromosomal theory of genetic inheritance. His experiments were famously conducted on *Drosophila melanogaster*, otherwise known as the fruit fly. This species, because of its rapid lifecycle, has been a favorite of genetic studies for a hundred years.[6]

Drosophila has four pairs of chromosomes (humans have 23 pairs) which makes it an easier species to study for chromosomal inheritance patterns than more complex species like humans. Moreover, Morgan was able to induce mutations that were single gene traits in fruit flies. Most biology students know of this study and Morgan's elation at producing his white-eyed fruit fly strain, which helped confirm the chromosome theory. He noted that certain traits followed the same chromosome related to gender, suggesting that the gene for the trait was present on the chromosome for the gender. As it turns out, there are a number of genetically inherited traits that are "sex-linked" owing to the presence of the genes on the chromosomes determining gender. Among such traits are hemophilia, Duchene muscular dystrophy and testicular feminization syndrome, to name just a few in humans. The discovery of the chromosomal linkage of inheritance marked a "honing in" on the molecular mechanism of genetics, which would eventually lead to uncovering the actual structure of DNA.[7]

Following Morgan's work, a number of researchers began to focus in on the molecular mechanism for heredity. In 1928, Frederick Griffith discovered that some sort of molecular information was preserved from virulent strains of *Streptococcus*, although dead, which could render live, non-virulent strains deadly. In 1944, Oswald Avery, C. M. MacLeod, and

M. McCarty narrowed down the molecule responsible for this "transform-ing principle" to DNA, which composes chromosomes, but which many still felt was too simple to carry the complex information comprising genes. DNA was known to have only four bases, and so was considered by many to simply be unlikely to be the genetic material capable of carrying all the complex information involved in developing organisms and main-taining their metabolism. Others favored proteins, which are composed of 20 amino acids, and which combine in tens of thousands of possible ways into complexly folded structures.[8]

Despite the Avery et al. experiments, it took experiments by Alfred Hershey and Martha Chase, in 1952, to convince most scientists that DNA was the molecular mechanism of heredity. Having reasoned that "phage"[9] infections produced the transformative effect observed by Avery et al., Hershey and Chase introduced a radioisotope of phosphorus (which exists naturally and non-radioactively in DNA but not proteins) into phage DNA, and a radioisotope of sulfur (which exists naturally and non-radioactively in proteins but not DNA) into another phage culture. They then infected *E. coli* with each phage culture, waited for injection of the phage DNA, then harvested the phage "shells" and measured the radioactive isotopes. They noted that the phosphorus-labeled phage shells had transmitted almost all of their phosphorus into the *E. coli*, whereas the sulfur-labeled phages maintained their radioactivity. They reasoned that DNA was thus the information-carrying molecule that carried the infection, producing transformation. Protein wasn't changing the *E. coli* phenotype, DNA was. It would take the famous team of Watson and Crick to begin to unravel the structure, and thus the mechanism for transmitting hereditary material in DNA, or genes, from one generation to the next.[10]

Jim Watson and Francis Crick met at Cambridge in 1951, convinced that DNA was the molecular mechanism for heredity. Watson was determined to unravel the structure of DNA, and he and Francis Crick began working on the problem using logic and then eventually models. They worked first from a number of known premises, including the work of Avery, Hershey and Chase. They also had a clue from the work of Erwin Chargaff, who discovered that the bases thymine and adenine always appeared in equal proportions, as did cytosine and guanine. They realized that the total amount of thymine plus cytosine was equal to the total amount of adenine and guanine. They began with an assumption about DNA's structure informed by Linus Pauling's work on the helical structure of certain pro-teins. Finally, they found Maurice Wilkins, of Kings College, who was doing x-ray spectroscopy work with Rosalind Franklin on crystallized DNA. Franklin's x-ray photos helped confirm the helical structure of DNA: the details of their methodology and inferences are well-chronicled, including in Watson's own account *The Double Helix*.[11] In sum, they realized that DNA had a double-helical structure, with base pairs arranged along rungs of a twisting ladder, all held together on a sugar and phosphate backbone. Each thymine was joined across the rung by an adenine, and each guanine paired with a cytosine. Thus, they inferred the mechanism of replication, later confirmed, by the unzipping of the ladder, leading to two complementary strands each of which served as a template for forming a new exact copy of the original genome.[12]

Inferring the structure of DNA opened the door for tremendous advances in understanding the role of genes in creating life, directing replication, and ongoing metabolic processes responsible for maintaining life at both the cellular and organism level. The Watson–Crick hypothesis posited a form of replication they called *semi-conservative*. Semi-conservative replication involves splitting of the double helix with enzymes into its component halves – the "parent" strand of DNA and creating two half-new daughter strands as living cells divided. Others proposed variants including *conservative* and *dispersive* models of replication. In 1958, Mathew Meselson and Franklin Stahl experimentally confirmed the semi-conservative model in *E. coli*.[13] In 1963, John Cairnes observed the predicted "replication zipper" or "fork" that forms as cells divide. The upshot of these discoveries was confirmation of the process by which cells divide while preserving the information for genetic inheritance, the method of adoption of parental traits during meiosis, and preserving the individual's genetic identity in all its cells as somatic cells undergo mitosis. Once this was discovered, all that remained was understanding what genes are, how they are expressed in the phenotype, and how they interrelate to the environment. We are only now beginning to answer these questions.

How Genes Work

Once scientists deduced that DNA was the genetic code they could begin to work on unraveling the precise mechanisms and meanings of that code in producing individual and species-wide phenotypes. A number of intermediary breakthroughs have brought us to the current state of affairs. We seem to understand the mechanism, but are still deciphering the code. Before even the structure of DNA was deduced, George Beadle and Edward Tatum proposed the "one-gene, one-enzyme" hypothesis. Working with the fungus *Neurospora*, they produced and isolated a number of mutant strains, each of which was unable to grow without the addition to the medium of some specific supplement. They noted, through chromosome staining, that the mutations responsible for different characters occurred on different locations of separate chromosomes, and that each mutation required the addition of specific nutrients. Their work would lead, once the biomechanical processes were uncovered, to what is now known as the "one-gene, one-enzyme" (or one protein) hypothesis. This hypothesis implies that biochemical processes of living cells occur in discrete processes, each of which is catalyzed by a specific enzyme, which is itself specified by a specific gene. In the Beadle–Tatum experiments, known mutations in genes produced predictable absences of certain enzymes. Only after Watson and Crick's breakthrough could scientists begin to understand the actual mechanisms of interactions among genes, enzymes and other proteins.[14]

We are made of proteins, and proteins interacting with their environments determine the structure of each of our organs and many of our unique traits as individuals. Genes control the production of enzymes and other proteins. Proteins are macromolecules made up of amino acids and the topology (shape) and composition of proteins is responsible for every organic process. All living things have proteins made from 20 common amino acids, which are joined in polypeptide chains (so-called because the amino acids are strung together by covalent peptide bonds), that can be as long as 1,000 or more amino acids. The "primary" structure of the protein is the linear string of amino acids. The "secondary" structure refers to the relationships of those amino acids that are close together in the linear polypeptide chain, often causing repeating patterns. The "tertiary" structure of proteins involves their three-dimensional structures, which are often complexly folded due to bonds among various amino acids. Complex proteins like hemoglobin (which in various forms comprises our blood) have quaternary structures that are *multimeric*, having numerous surfaces, and involving the combination of several separate polypeptide chains.[15]

The shape and linear sequence of a protein results in its function given that certain sites are available for certain substrates to bond and certain reactions to thus catalyze. Genes direct the creation of every protein, thus directing every biological function of every organism. The complexity of proteins and their structures convinced many scientists early on to believe they were the carriers of genetic data, but as it turns out, they only do the bidding of genes which direct their creation and action in every cell of every organ of every living creature. In 1957, Vernon Ingram discovered that changes in the structures of hemoglobin proteins resulted from mutations in genes, and the entire structure and function of hemoglobin could be harmfully altered by a single substitution of a single amino acid in the two polypeptide chains composing hemoglobin alpha and beta. That single substitution, of the amino acid valine for that of glutamic acid at a single point in the chain results in sickle cells, a known hereditary disease. Working with *E. coli*, Charles Yanofsy demonstrated the correlation between gene sequence and amino acid sequence, and thus how mutated genes cause various traits, including harmful mutations.[16]

Yanofsky mapped genes and found a direct correlation between the sequence of mutational sites and altered amino acids, or *colinearity* between the linear sequence of the gene and polypeptide structure and thus function. In fact, the Mendelian notion of dominance and recessiveness makes sense with an understanding of how genes direct enzymes and other proteins.[17] Simply put, most dominant traits involve the presence of enzyme function, whereas recessiveness involves the absence of enzyme function. But how do genes direct this complex process, creating proteins by causing amino acids to join in specified sequences, all while sitting comfortably and relatively statically (except during mitosis) inside the nuclei of cells? It's a complex dance, involving DNA and some other helpful molecules, and directing nearly every biomechanical function of every organism on earth.

DNA Function in Metabolism

DNA functions as a sort of information storage device in the nuclei of cells, and also as the core of a kind of Central Processing Unit (CPU), guiding the production of proteins in the cytoplasm, the space outside the nucleus in cells. For this, it relies upon the help of its sister molecule: RNA. Early experiments with radioactively-labeled RNA showed that it moved quickly from the nucleus to the cytoplasm (the stuff surrounding the nucleus), where it was known that proteins are synthesized. Elliot Volkin and Lawrence Astrachan discovered in 1957 that RNA introduced via phages into *E. coli* nuclei rapidly moved into the cytoplasm. The three phases of its metabolism were shown to be 1 replication, by which RNA is synthesized in the nucleus from DNA, 2 transcription, by which a portion of DNA is synthesized into an RNA copy (uracil replaces thymine in RNA), and finally 3 translation, which is the synthesis of a polypeptide directed by the RNA sequence.[18]

There are genetic signals, regions called "promoters" that are known codes on DNA which modulate transcription by signaling RNA polymerase, the enzyme responsible for transcribing RNA, to begin or end the task. It ends when it reaches the signal for termination. We are beginning to see how complex DNA is as we delve into these processes. Because it is both information storage and CPU, it includes processing signals, as well as core information. Somewhat like an ingenious natural Turing machine,[19] it directs all these processes by means of helpful molecules that read its code *and* do its work. Essentially, RNA comes in several forms, including "messenger" and "transfer" that move the instructions for protein synthesis from the nuclei to the ribosomes, which are organelles in the cellular cytoplasm where proteins are finally synthesized. The code for all this is stored in *codons*, which are the smallest meaningful units of information in DNA. Codons are three-base long units of DNA, each of which codes for the production of a specific amino acid. The language of DNA is "degenerate" because it contains more than enough words for each of the 20 amino acids. Given three-letter words, and four letters that may compose them, there are 64 possible three-letter words. In fact, each amino acid can be made by a number of different "words," or codons. Thus, the amino acid *His* (histidine) is signaled by either CAU (remember, uracil stands in for thymine in RNA), or CAC. As well, there are words that are promoters and inhibitors – signals that tell the RNA to start or stop transcribing.[20]

The ribosome is the cellular factory that fabricates polypeptides from the basic amino acids according to the instructions delivered to it by RNA. It is these polypeptides that then, based upon their specific geometries and topologies, carrying on the tasks of metabolism, ensure the continued functioning and specific traits of each individual organism. So, how do specific cell types know which traits to express? In other words, since the DNA in every cell is identical, carrying the exact same information as in every other cell of that organism, how do liver cells know not to become eyes? Why do arms not start digesting things like stomachs do? The answer is, through differentiation.

Differentiation

Each somatic cell (except for blood cells) carries the entire code of the organism in its nucleus. But each somatic cell type looks and acts distinctly, performing specialized functions, producing distinct proteins, expressing different organs depending on where it resides in the body. The instructions that cause them to do this, to function distinctly, and express various particular organs, functions, and processes are themselves part of the entire genome, only part of which is expressed according to that cell's organ, function, and process.

DNA regulates its expression in differentiated cells by repressing genes controlling enzymes that are unnecessary for their functioning as part of a particular process or organ. Expression of particular proteins is regulated by a combination of mechanisms, including *repressor* proteins, which bind to the portion of a gene called the *operator*. The repressor prevents transcription by RNA polymerase by binding to the operator, inhibiting the *promoter* sequence which would ordinarily cause RNA polymerase to begin transcription of its *operon*. Sometimes, cells need to alter their function, and express functions that were previously inhibited. This process is called *induction* and often involves a feedback loop, so that, for instance, organs which produce things like lactose in mammals do so only when necessary, when inducers go to work and turn off repressors. The process of gene expression regulation was first begun to be understood by Francois Jacob and Jacques Monod, who discovered that a particular substrate of inducers augmented the production of specific enzymes. Their experiments showed that differentiated cells turned on and off gene expression according to various environmental signals. In the process of their experiments, they found that certain genes were *coordinately controlled*, so that, for instance, the gene controlling the production of an enzyme worked in conjunction with the gene controlling the transport of that enzyme.[21]

There are numerous such control mechanisms that work to coordinate gene expression throughout organisms. Some do so developmentally, so that cells in the body differentiate into liver, or bone, or whatever type of cell is appropriate for the place in the body the cell is in as the organism develops. Others turn on and off functions according to environmental conditions. Some exhibit feedback inhibition, ensuring that certain enzymes are always present in specific quantities or concentrations. Some repressors inhibit only one operator, while others control several. In sum, gene expression control is a complicated form of information processing by which cells in the body are prevented from expressing all of their genes at once, even while each cell contains all of the information for expression of every gene responsible for each facet of the organism's existence.

Information, Structure and Function: Individuals and "Persons"

It is not an exaggeration to say as I have above that the genome, interacting with its environment, is a sort of very complex Turing machine. It codes information enough to conduct every single process, from development through metabolism and reproduction, all with the aide of other molecules, including enzymes, various forms of RNA, proteins and the inter- and intra-cellular environments, all of which are likewise coordinated by the information encoded in the organism's DNA. It is the structure of DNA that enables it to direct all other functions and processes throughout the organism, as well as to replicate both from one generation to the next, and within the body as necessary to perpetuate both the species and the indi-vidual. The ultimate form of an organism is directed at the molecular level by the sequence of bases with input from the environment. There are nu-merous and ongoing intermediate steps from the level of the basic informa-tion to expression in the form of the organism, and various opportunities for things to go wrong. In other words, each organism has its prototypical form, as expressed in the bulk of its members, and its particular form, as expressed by its particular genetic makeup in combination with the environment. Some individuals exhibit pathological features. This is a good juncture to get clear on some terms and concepts that will recur, and which cause actual confusion in other discussions of these ideas: namely, "expression" and "environment."

"Expression" is not an Expression

Ordinarily, the term "expression" connotes intention. For instance, I have argued that all man-made objects intentionally produced are expressions and vice-versa. Thus, it is technically inaccurate to discuss biological phenomena, which are typically not the result of human intention (except through genetic engineering) as somehow "expressions." Yet this is the biological terminology. It would be more philosophically accurate to call the phenotype and its features "end-results" of the genotype rather than expressions, because an end-result does not imply teleology (intention). Throughout this text, however, we will use the typical biological term and ignore its troubling philosophical implication except when otherwise necessary for the argument.

Genes and "Environment"

Genes and environments are inseparable. Genes do not exist absent environments, and so when we discuss DNA, genes, and their expressions via phenotypes, we must always remember that environments shape the expression of genes. Namely, organisms exist in environments that shape their existence just as necessarily as do their genes. The particular form of the individual depends necessarily on being provided by its environment with certain necessary nutrients, media, and energy in various forms. There is a one-way ontological dependence therefore among genes and environments. The latter do not depend in any necessary way upon genes, although the environment we know is constantly being shaped and changed by organisms and their genes.

Information and Individuals

A major mistake of most who have considered the ethics of ownership of DNA and its components has been to assume something about the relations of DNA, genes, information, and "expression" of genes in an *individual* in a certain environment in light of the biological terms as commonly used. Yet we can see by even a cursory look at the science of those relations that ordinary terms that frame much of the discussion of these concepts do not mean the same things in the context of the genome. Many assume blithely that DNA's "information" is like other forms of information, and its "expression" like other forms of expression, and thus the laws and treatment of DNA reflect typical forms of information protection in the law.

I have described the science above so that we can begin at the beginning, understanding first the basic ontology, or the relations among the composite parts of individuals and species, before leaping to conclusions about the *rights*, *duties* and other obligations owed or not owed to those *persons* whose genomes may be used for profit.

There are two parallel ontologies that will ultimately need to be reconciled to devise some sort of argument for or against the ownership of DNA. The first is the hierarchy and relations among atoms, molecules, DNA, RNA, enzymes and other proteins, cellular processes, biological functions, and other elements of the ongoing project contemplated by the Gene Ontology and related sciences.[22] The second is the social ontology of individuals, species, persons, and other socially relevant objects. Only *persons* are afforded rights and duties, including rights and duties concomitant with ownership as a social and legal institution. Thus, there must be some link or relationship between these two ontologies to conclude this analysis. For now, let's begin to consider the problem of the relations between DNA and individuals, which are less problematic than *persons*, as revealed by the scientific discussion above.

Individuals are not necessarily *persons*, but rather simply distinct tokens of the type represented by a species. Each individual organism is wholly unique, with both a distinct history to that individual's life, and unique genetic make-up. In the case of identical twins, the identical genetic make-up does not undo the unique individual history of each twin, and so there still exist two individuals. It is also statistically *possible* though incredibly improbable, that unrelated individuals of a species could share identical genetic make-up. Nonetheless, their unique histories would entitle each to their status as individuals. Individuals are also typically denoted by unique positions in space, with no two individuals overlapping. Complications arise for conjoined twins, who may share both DNA and space to a certain degree. Surely, each of a pair of conjoined twins has a sense of "me-ness" distinct from that of his or her twin. Conjoined twins are sometimes surgically separated, resulting in two more distinct individuals. Without getting into a long discussion of higher-order features such as those required by theories of *personhood*, we can say for now that each of a pair of conjoined twins does indeed have its own unique history of *experience* based upon *some degree* of separation from its twin. Thus, one twin was asleep while the other was not, and had a particular thought, emotion, experience, or perception separate and apart from that of its twin at some point.

Not every individual organism is a person, as some individuals are born dead, or never achieve some of the typical higher-order functioning associated with personhood. Moreover, most individuals are not human beings, and personhood, with all of the associated moral status associated with it, is reserved for only certain types of individuals.

Individualization is certainly connected with the information contained in the particular genetic code of each individual organism. That information alone, however, is necessary but insufficient for declaring an organism to be an individual person given the case of identical twins and statistically improbable but possible sharing of identical genetic code with unrelated others. We can think of individuals as continuants overlapping with their particular occurrent life-histories. This overlap is important because the individual is more than just the genetic information or unique spatio-temporal location, but also all of the developmental and experiential steps preceding any particular moment of that individual, as in the case of the conjoined twins. The elements of those unique histories include all of the biological processes described above, both developmentally and metaboli-cally, that occurred to create the present form of each individual. The geno-type is only a partial blueprint for the individual, with environment and history playing large roles as well.

Much of an individual's genome is in fact shared among all others of the species, with only a relatively small fraction unique to the individual. Thus, a relevant line of questioning we should also consider is, to what extent do the elements of the genome shared in common with the rest of the species belong to us as individuals, or to the species as a whole, or for that matter, to anyone at all? We will also need to ask to what extent that part of the genome particular to an individual may be properly claimed as owned by anyone, under what conditions, and under what conceptual framework? These questions all depend to some degree on discerning the relations among individuals, persons, their "selves," and their bodies and materials parts. Finally, we will eventually need to come back to the problem of *persons* and their relation to the genome.

Personhood and "Me-ness"

In order to work out whether there is any moral connection to one's genetic code, we must work out the status of the relationships among the code itself, its "expression" in individuals, and ultimately in persons. The ontological status of individuals is only part of the puzzle. The real hard work is deciding when individuals become rights-bearing persons, and then to what extent they have rights, if any, over their own genome or that part of the genome shared in common among all individuals.

Persons are the relevant entities for moral considerations, as discussed previously, rather than individuals, organisms, or even simply human beings. Both the law and ethics have distinguished historically among persons and other sorts of entities. Only persons have been traditionally treated as bearing rights or owing duties. The term "person" represents a social object recognized by legal and moral codes, but not inherent in the "brute-fact" object itself. Social objects are created by "collective intentionality," or agreements among communities. The status of *personhood* is not synonymous with the "brute-fact" object *human*. Humans are the biological entities, and while they are generally composed of the same matter as all known and recognized *persons*, being a person requires certain capacities. These capacities typically include some level of cognition including at least the potential for reasoning, awareness, intentionality, and the like. Both laws and moral codes treat persons as special – as objects requiring moral and legal consideration, and as capable of moral and legal culpability. Hopefully, understanding these objects and their relations will clarify some of the mistakes made so far in categorizing genes and DNA, and help us to devise policies that are more just and ethical.

There is no doubt that there is an ontological dependence of the person and the individual on the genome and on the scientific facts described above. At one level, each depends on the common genome (that part of the genome we use to classify a species, and the traits, functions, processes, and structures common to all members of the species). At the next level, each individual and person depends ontologically on the existence of *its particular* genome, the exact string of bases coordinating its particular development and metabolism. Many would be tempted to declare then that the person and individual are synonymous with the string of DNA particular to that individual or person. But this would be a gross oversimplification of the ontology, and a mischaracterization of the science. Our current understanding of DNA undermines the notion of absolute genetic determinism. As mentioned above, DNA does not exist isolated from its environment. In fact, the emerging view of *epigenetics* places a significant importance on the role of the environment in shaping the development of individuals.[23] This is due to the ongoing role of DNA in development and metabolism. The blueprint (DNA) informs development according to materials available (the environment), and the environment continues to inform metabolism even after development. Genes switch on and off based on cues from the environment. The individual thus never becomes "fixed" and continues to function in various ways based upon feedback from the individual's environment.

So what part of the genome is "me?" and how much of *my* genome is "mine?" We will return to this fundamental question and its relation to the problem of *persons* after a more thorough analysis of the relationships among genomes, species, and individuals in the next chapter.

4 DNA, SPECIES, INDIVIDUALS, AND PERSONS

The sciences of genetics and genomics are revealing more all the time regarding our statuses as individuals relative to our particular genomes. The more we learn about our individual genetic uniqueness relative to one another within the human species, the more it appears likely that individuality is tied strongly and very intricately to our genes as well as our environments. The law of property and ownership, as well as emerging notions of autonomy and privacy, hinge both historically and rationally upon notions of individuality. Let's look at some of the scientific and genetic bases for individuality, and relate it if we can to implications for self-ownership and gene patenting.

There is a substantial body of philosophical discussion and debate regarding the nature of individual persons and consciousness, considering questions about the roles of minds, brains, and consciousness in defining ourselves as individuals. Our concern here is with DNA and genes, and how they either define the individual or otherwise relate to individuals. These questions are related to questions about the nature of property and other rights over other sorts of objects. For instance, in intellectual property law, there is a clear distinction between the ownership rights granted under patent and copyright laws to types (species) rather than tokens (individuals). The law of real property and of moveables differs from that of intellectual property, tracking both philosophical and practical distinctions among their objects relating to notions of individuality.

Underlying our decisions about rights over various forms of property is a distinction between types and tokens. Tokens are individuals, and types are universals. Both types and tokens may be "owned" in different ways, but under different legal schemes, and for agreed-upon philosophical reasons. Thus, I can sell my record collection (a collection of tokens each of which represents some type) without infringing the authors' rights to the types (the songs themselves). Similarly, I can sell or give away other sorts of property, such as machines or other utilitarian objects protected under patent law, without violating the patent right. I cannot myself make tokens from the types because unauthorized reproduction is forbidden. This brings up all sorts of very interesting and troubling concerns regarding the current regime of patent protection for unmodified genes or other natural genetic products where ownership is clamed over the *information* (types) expressed by the genes or the entire genome of an organism.

If you own a patent, you exclusively have the right to make tokens representing the type that you invented. Anyone who makes unauthorized tokens of your patented type must pay you if you sue them and the court finds they infringed your patent. Being the first to have filed a patent on a type makes you the prima facie owner of the patent against all late-comers. If you own a patent on a gene, then no one may reproduce the type in any token without paying you royalties. Ownership of the type in patent law is really an exclusionary device preventing others from making tokens of the type owned. Since unmodified (or wild-type) genes propagate throughout the natural world, often in numerous species, individual tokens are constantly being reproduced without anyone having any intent to infringe on anyone's patent. This happens constantly and outside the realm of any reasonable control by the patent holder. No other sort of ownable object does this in quite this way. In other words, while you might own a particular sheep, you cannot own every sheep in the world by virtue of a claim over the type – *sheep*. If you have successfully filed a patent over a non-engineered sheep gene, however, you suddenly *do* become the owner of at least a *part* of every new and existing sheep in the world. This is a state of affairs that simply could not exist for hammers or steam engines because they do not reproduce themselves, they require human intention to produce them.

In the law of ownership claims over types and tokens, we can see how philosophical notions of individuality and uniqueness strongly relate to decisions we make about legal rules for ownership and reproduction. How do these notions apply to genes and genomes, and do scientific concepts of genetic individuals and species help inform us in making rational and just policies regarding gene patenting or self-ownership?

Individuals and Species

The set of members of a species existing contemporaneously define the category species, and thus, in some ways the biological classification of a particular species is always vague. Species change over time and *speciate*, requiring taxonomists to classify the new species as something separate from the prior species, although the individuals composing the new species are all seamlessly related to the prior species. All species are composed of some critical population of individuals, all of whom share some important features, and yet each of which differs from each other both phenotypically and genotypically. The puzzling nature of individuals and species, their relations to each other and to the social object "person," are central issues ignored for the most part in discussions regarding the nature of any rights over genes or other DNA products. We must at least acknowledge these important issues even if we cannot entirely solve them here.

A *species* is a complex object, defined by its constituents, and bounded temporally. It exists as something both bounded by certain biological facts in a snapshot of time (as a continuant), and as an occurent bounded over a span of time. Its boundaries are necessarily vague, though its members at any one time are generally not. Evolutionary theory and the present state of genetic science suggest that all life on earth has a common ancestor and thus a common origin. Over time, geographical isolation and environmental pressures on populations of that common ancestor selected for various mutations over others, resulting in speciation so that some generations of offspring of the common ancestor were no longer sufficiently similar to one another to be considered members of the same species. This process was accelerated with the development of sexual reproduction, which creates greater genetic diversity of offspring than does parthenogenesis. Sexual reproduction ensures that offspring are more distinctly individuals in the sense that their genotypes are much more significantly different from their parents than in the case of parthenogenetic division.[1] When amoebas reproduce by splitting, it's a fair question as to which two individuals result is the parent and which is the offspring. There's no good philosophical answer to this problem as each half is a fully formed individual that resulted from an original individual which then ceases to exist. Fortunately for us, sexual reproduction makes determining the individuality of parents and offspring much less tricky.

When we say that a species is defined by its constituents, we acknowledge that all current members of a species are sufficiently similar so that they can all interbreed, which is actually logically necessary for that species to perpetuate – to survive. Being able to interbreed is also logically necessary for that species to eventually evolve into another species. This seems to be a sort of paradox, because at some point, in classical slippery slope fashion, a new species evolves, although at any one time only one species seems to exist. In fact, this is often a naïve objection raised by opponents of evolutionary theory who claim that the process of speciation has never been observed and thus cannot be claimed to be an observed phenomenon of evolution. Of course, speciation can be observed only in contrast with other existing species that are far enough removed on the evolutionary tree so that interbreeding no longer occurs, or at least does not produce fertile offspring. Witness, for instance, donkeys and horses, which are indeed different species, incapable of producing fertile offspring, but nonetheless sufficiently recently speciated so that they can still interbreed and produce sterile mules. Members of recently diverged species share significant enough genetic similarities so that they can sometimes produce offspring, but generally are unable to do so, or may produce only sterile or otherwise deficient offspring. This is the operative definition of speciation.[2]

Geographical isolation is presumably the greatest factor in allowing for populations of a species to change genetically over time, in response to environmental pressures and genetic drift accelerated by the mechanism of sexual reproduction. Dramatic examples of speciation due to these factors can be observed by looking at island-isolated species such as Madagascar's lemurs, or the success of marsupials on Australia and Tasmania. Geographical isolation, environmental pressures, and genetic drift took those populations in dramatically different paths than their ancestral relatives in different environments and localities. In fact, it was the same factors that resulted in the famous observations of speciation of finches and other species in the Galapagos Islands as observed by Charles Darwin in the mid nineteenth century. In his *Origins of Species*, Darwin notes that even minor geographical isolation and slightly different environmental pressures result in subtle changes in physiology and even speciation.[3]

At any one time a species exists and is distinct from some relative but non-specific timeframe in which the predecessor species existed. Were the two species (the predecessor and the later) co-existent in time, they would not be able to inter-breed successfully and thus they would be considered separate species. Sometimes, predecessor species diverge into two concurrent, related, but distinct species that meet these criteria. Chimpanzees and humans diverged from some common predecessor species more than 5 million years ago. Tracing back through these two species' DNA reveals an almost identical genetic identity still, so that the two current species share 96 percent of their DNA.[4] During some time-span, there was a single predecessor species to both chimps and humans, but geography and environmental pressures caused subtle changes in populations over time, causing enough divergence eventually to properly call each a separate species.

Commonalities among Species

Even though members of a species are generally incapable of breeding successfully outside their species, there are significant similarities among all species that become more pronounced among closely related species. In a sense, each individual belongs to several categories at once, including: member of a family of direct lineage (fathers, mothers, siblings), member of an extended family (uncles, cousins), tribal units consisting of related families (generally not recognized in the developed world), and so on. All humans are related to one another through a common ancestor that lived just a few thousand years ago and everyone alive now is hundredth-cousins at the very most to any other person.[5] Moreover, many of our genes, as well as introns and pseudogenes (genetic code that appears not to be directly responsible for any one enzyme or protein but still seems to be somehow vital to survival) are shared even among distantly separated species. It is this fact that makes genetic engineering feasible. It has also helped significantly in identifying specific human genes. Because genes had been identified in organisms as simple as fruit flies, and their functions were known precisely, the first work in identifying some functions of human genes during the course of the Human Genome Project was accelerated by looking for genes known to have certain functions in other species.[6] Genes known to direct the production of hemoglobin in mice, for instance, are substantially the same in humans and other mammals.

The fact that genes carry over from species to species does not mean that those genes are completely identical across all species, however. Even within members of the same species there is some variation among genes. Genetics are certainly important in speciation, and some threshold of genetic similarity must be involved, if for no other reason than that that genetic similarity is responsible for other phenotypical, morphological, or environmental factors of speciation. Commonality of genes is often used alongside the standard definition of species coined by Ernst Mayr, called the biological or isolation species concept, which states that species are: "groups of actually or potentially interbreeding natural populations which are reproductively isolated from other such groups."[7] Add to this the notion that at some point isolated species are no longer capable of interbreeding successfully because their genotypes become sufficiently distinct, and we begin to get a picture of the precise difficulty of fixing the notion of speciation in any one time, place, or for our purposes, *individual.* Nonetheless, one could draft a "tree" of life, trace it back to microbial precursors of every other life form, and at least note that species do at some point diverge into branches. The individuals, we could say, are the leaves.

Discerning the relations among the leaves, the branches, and the tree (so to speak) is essential because, as discussed briefly in previous chapters, we are concerned with human *persons* when deciding on the ethics of our behaviors. Which is not to say that we don't have certain norms or taboos concerning the treatment of other species, as well as enlightened self-interest, or bona-fide ethical reasons to treat the environment in such-and-such a way as well. However, the bulk of our moral and ethical codes concern how we treat fellow members of our species. Without yet getting into the question of whether such codes, norms, or systems of ethics *ought* to be extended to other branches on the earth's tree of life, we will need to decide what relations the human genome has to the genomes of other species, which we manipulate, own, or otherwise treat in ways we would not treat other humans.

There must be some sound reason to distinguish the proper bearers of most rights – human persons – as members of the human species distinct from chimps, for instance, despite their substantial genetic similarities. Yet, human individuals are also significantly, if not as substantially, different from one another, as individual bearers of particular genomes, and yet all are considered part of the same species, and, if *persons,* proper bearers of human rights. We need to isolate the reasons for the ethical significance of dissimilarities among humans and among species in order to justify our use of other species to various degrees, and any reasons or limits we might seek to justify on the use of other humans. We will also need to distinguish acceptable uses as either justifiable trespasses on tokens (individuals – for instance, by animal experimentation, or on other human persons when done with adequate consent) and types (the use of the "genotypes" or unique "genes" of a species).

We can see that species and individual organisms are all interrelated historically, and over time develop differences significant enough to consider them no longer bearers of certain statuses. There are promising theories in evolutionary psychology as to the adaptive advantages of the development of these new statuses, but we need not delve into them.[8] It is sufficient for our purposes to acknowledge that members of a species acknowledge fellow species-members as distinct from members of other species. We do this as humans through laws which recognize the personhood of other humans, and in ethical codes which, for the most part, apply only within the species. We do this despite the fact that we share genes with other species. So how do we justify treating individuals within species as bearers of rights, and objects of duties, when each of us is in some sense a transitional instance between predecessor and future divergent species? What makes us so special as a species first, and as individuals and ultimately persons within that species?

Individuals within Species

In order to develop a robust account of what rights individual members of the human species might have to either their own particular DNA, or to the human genome in general, we need to explain the relations between individuals and species in regards to DNA. In sum, there is a species-wide genome, which both defines the species and is defined by the species' members for a certain stretch of time. The exact time periods for the existence of a species cannot be known absolutely, and are noted only in retrospect by taxonomists and biologists. This is because the genetic differences between members of a particular species and some predecessor species are what account for speciation, and no one particular generation "becomes" the next species . . . it is a gradual, vague occurrence.

Most of the human genome seems to be non-functioning. At least, it isn't responsible for directing the production of proteins. Only 1.5 percent of the three billion base pairs of human DNA encodes proteins.[9] A similar percentage appears to direct the process of reading the proteins encoding genes. This leaves a huge percentage of apparently non-coding "junk DNA" that typically resembles other functioning genes, but lacks promoters or other control sequences. Scientists theorize that these are once-useful byproducts of evolution. Many of these regions are filled with large swaths of repeating introns that may yet code information important for metabolism and reproduction somehow.

Given that such a small percentage of our DNA seems to actually be active, with that roughly 1.5 percent encoding the nearly 100,000 proteins involved in our development and metabolism, and a similar percentage serving as essentially reading instructions for various processes, we might expect a large degree of similarity among individuals. All of that junk DNA and pseudogenes left over from hundreds of millions of years of evolution should not matter much in individuating humans from each other. Isn't it the stuff that actually does things all that matters? Not necessarily.

As it turns out, we are discovering that so-called junk DNA and pseudogenes are responsible for more differences among individuals than we would either expect or can even currently explain. When the Human Genome Project was completed, attention was turned to mapping single-nucleotide polymorphisms (SNPs) in the HapMap project. The overall picture given by the HGP was the terrain of the active genes and promoter regions, in which SNPs were believed to be responsible for variations in human traits. Life turns out to be more complicated than this, however. Variations in pseudogenes, junk DNA and "copy-number variants" (CNVs, which are large sections of the genome of healthy human beings that are either missing or duplicated) abound, and may be involved in phenotypic differences such as susceptibility to diseases. This has been discovered through a recent project designed to map CNVs. These tend to occur in sections of DNA located near cross-over points during replication, and scientists have learned these CNVs may account for as much as 12 percent of the human genome. Some 1,400 CNVs have so far been detected, and result in much greater variability among individuals of the human species than previously suspected.[10] According to Charles Lee of the Harvard Medical School, "[t]his evidence is showing that we are more genetically unique from one another – we all have individualized genomes."

Our individuality is the result of at least two interacting forces: 1 our individualized genomes, and 2 our individual histories. And yet, we share, together with other species, a common history of genetic evolution. Any account of genetic and historical individuality must also account for our shared biological past. Richard Dawkins described all life on earth as arising out of a flowing river of genes, with species existing as forks in that river.[11] On this metaphor, perhaps individual members of a species are the ripples on that river, flashing in and out of existence, giving birth to new ripples, varying widely, but appearing similar to each other.

Our genetic identities, combined with our individual histories, make us unique in more fundamental ways than do, for instance, our appearances, our fingerprints, or even our dreams, thoughts, hopes or wishes, because all of the latter derive in large part from the former. If we are the custodians or owners of other aspects of our individuality, then by what account are we not at least intimately connected to our individual genomes? Moreover, as individuals in the genetic river of humanity, does the human genome connect us one to another, and to other species, in ways that defy property law or other moral duties and obligations to one another and perhaps ourselves? Before we consider these critical questions, let's first look at the historical and genetic significance of our individual identities.

Individual Histories and Individual Genomes

While it is improper to equate an individual with his or her genome alone, the facts regarding the range of differences, and the phenotypic results of those differences, make each individual's specific genome at least a very *important* part of individual identity. Moreover, individual identity is also at least partly ontologically dependent (i.e., the dependent object would not exist without the other object) upon individual genomic uniqueness. But each living individual also has a unique history that determines in large part the element of individual identity we often equate with personhood. More than the biomechanical processes responsible for an organism's mere functioning, social and cultural designations of relevant higher-level functions combine to form the social object "person" that makes certain acts and intentions directed toward other human persons moral or immoral, prohibited or permitted. But individuality precedes personhood, and even non-human organisms, and human non-persons (like corpses, for instance), remain individuals due as much to their histories as to their genetic uniqueness.

Consider the example of twins. As discussed previously, twins share genetic identities, yet they are clearly individuals. Set aside for the moment any notion of internal mental states, or consciousness, and assume non-person twins, without consciousness or any hope thereof. Each genetically identical twin would nonetheless share a unique history, making each an individual, beginning with their unique positions in space. Even conjoined twins do not share every portion of their bodies with one another, though they share part. Setting aside for the moment the likelihood that the seat of the most essential elements of personhood, the brain of each conjoined twin, is separate (though they might share certain neural pathways), the separation of even a part of each makes each a distinct individual inasmuch as they each have their own parts or features. Prior to twinning, which takes place typically within the first two weeks of development, twins were in fact a single individual, though as we will discuss below, not yet likely considered *persons*. When twinning occurs, a single individual becomes two, or three, or however many genetically identical copies result.

Spatio-temporal location accounts for notions of individuation in every medium. Thus, the design specs and blueprint for a type of widget manufactured in quantities, each member of which is supposed to be identical to the other, represent the model for each widget, but each widget necessarily occupies a unique spatio-temporal position that no other widget, no matter how identical it may seem to another, may occupy. Keep in mind that when speaking about widgets, or texts, selling or giving away a token (or individual) does not result in parting with the type. Under copyright and patent law, the rights to the type remain with the author or inventor. Individual widgets or works of authorship may represent similar or even identical types and yet remain distinct from both the type and every other token. There are no two individuals that occupy exactly the same space-time. There are no two individuals that are identical.[12]

For now, and without implying any intentionality, let's call the spatio-temporal path of any individual its "life-path." The life-path of each individual widget is determined by factors outside its apparent control. The life-path of a person owes something, however, to the person's intentions. The life-path of a widget is also determined in part due to its design and function, so that most every chair occupies some floor space somewhere and likely gets sat upon at some time. The life-paths of organisms are also determined in part by their evolved features and functions. As of yet, for instance, no terrestrial organism occupies a vacuum well because, if it happens to try, it generally dies. Birds don't breathe water and fish don't perch in trees. The life-paths of species as wholes determine in large part the life-paths of individuals within those species, and each individual, occupying its own unique spatio-temporal location, ends up pursuing a life-path unique to itself, with certain limitations.

An important part of each organism's unique history is determined by its unique genome, as well as to the genome it shares with other members of that species. Thus, two individuals may smoke equal amounts in their lifetimes, and one may contract cancer while the other one may die of old age. Some genetically identical twins even exhibit unique expression of traits, so that it sometime happens that one twin may appear healthy in all respects, and the other may develop Tourettes or other psychological, cognitive or physical impairments despite apparently identical genetics. The science of epigenetics may help to explain how one's genotype is only part of the making of an individual's uniqueness and the importance of history or life-path to each individual. Exposure to various environmental conditions sometimes triggers or suppresses expression of various genes. Thus, each organism's unique life-path is a formative element of genetic identity in important ways. Moreover, history is formative of the *person*, as well as the individual. More on persons shortly.

The Social and Legal Importance of Individuality

Why does individual uniqueness matter? We clearly place a good deal of emphasis on individuality in the things we consider capable of being possessed and, more importantly, owned. We value less those tangible things that are abundant and value more those things that are rare. Those things that are truly "one of a kind" are often our most prized possessions and are sometimes quite expensive and valuable as well. Some of these things are valuable because of the specific intentionality put into their making, such as authentic Fabergé eggs (vs. fake ones). Some unique natural things are valuable simply due to their rarity, such as meteorites. Other things are valued due to cultural or social norms associated with them, such as diamonds (which are valued more than their numbers or rarity would seem to warrant). Values are not inherent in objects, and valuing is the result of a complex web of intentionality and desire. But natural facts may account for part of the value of an object, such as the natural facts of an object's rarity. Thus, rare elements are often valued more than abundant ones, though not necessarily prized equally by everyone. When human intentionality creates things that become prized, there is typically more to our valuing than mere rarity. The art world is full of examples of one-of-a-kind yet worthless objects.

The natural world is a better example of one-to-one correspondence of unique individuals and value. Rare elements, such as gold and platinum, are valued in part due to their beauty, but also valued in themselves as rare natural elements. Meteorites are a similar example whose rarity imbues value in itself (well, at least in the first instance for human purposes, since nature values nothing) with additional states of affairs, such as beauty and scientific use increasing value. Oddly, all this valuing we've been discussing is separate and apart from any notion of necessity. One could make the argument that the most valuable things we come into contact with are food, water, and air. This is a tremendously important part of our discussion of rarity, uniqueness, and value relating to the social institutions of ownership.

Not only do we value food, water, and air differently, but we treat them differently in property regimes. Food, water, and air are treated as *fungibles*, meaning that any quantity of each is treated as equally interchangeable with the same quantity of the same type of thing (one pound of wheat is the same as any other pound of wheat, for example). Each is also exchangeable with the fair market price of that quantity of item as well. Meaning, for instance, that if you have a basket of food and I take it, and replace it with a basket of food with quantities and qualities identical to the former, you have no moral or legal claim against me. The same goes for an exchange of an identical quantity of water, or air if one can picture a suitable circumstance. Moreover, if I replace a quantity of a fungible item with money at the fair market price of that item, I have also not deprived you of anything. The money can be used to replace the goods, and each party in the exchange is left whole, with no property rights impeded or infringed. Food is generally considered fully fungible, and the net effect and meaning of this is that no particular item of food is treated as sufficiently unique that it cannot be replaced. Fungible items can be freely traded for amounts of other fungible items of an equal value at fair market price. Money itself is fungible, so that if I take from your wallet $10, and replace it with another $10, you have been deprived of nothing and have no claim against me for depriving you of something (although I would have likely invaded a privacy right in the contents of your wallet).

Nonfungible goods include most other *moveables* and *real property*. Moveables include any nonfungible property that is not land. "Real property" generally refers to land and improvements upon land. A theft of a moveable cannot be made right by its replacement with even an apparently identical moveable. If I decide that I prefer your car to mine, even though in all respects they may appear identical, and so I switch one for the other, I have violated your property interests in your particular car. How does a car differ from potato? Inherently, each is a unique spatio-temporal object, with its own particular history. Each is an individual. In fact, the fungible item, the potato, is arguably *more* unique than at least a production-line automobile, as there are typically numerous identical copies of cars. However, each potato is completely unique at least in its particular form, with eyes, imperfections, colorations, weights, densities, etc., unique to that particular potato. Yet the car is not fungible, and replacing one car with an identical one still results legally, and culturally, in a different sort of loss than replacing one potato with another.

One source for the non-fungibility of certain things may be that they are products of human intention. An automobile is not a naturally occurring product, whereas potatoes, water and air are. This is partly true, however most foods today, while still fungible, are in fact at least generally (as types) the products of human intention through selective breeding and the institutions and practice of agriculture. Cash is also the product of human intention. Rather, the intentionality that results in the fungibility of an object rests in the prospective *consumer*, not the producer. For instance, food *can* become non-fungible if valued for certain purposes or functions. A slice of wedding cake, frozen or otherwise preserved, is an irreplaceable object not because of the chemical make-up of the cake, but rather for the new function it has attained. Similarly, a coin collection, although it may be composed entirely of coins of legal tender, may attain non-fungible status due once again to the function for which the owner of the collection intends the coins, each of which may still be fungible. Critical to the new status of a fungible good turned non-fungible is the individuality of the object. Some new layer of individuality is acquired by such objects due to the person valuing them, whether that person is the owner, society, or any combination of these. Individuality is thus not something that inheres entirely in objects, but rather something that can be added upon, increased, changed, or otherwise influenced by human intentions.

Individuality increases relative value. The mixing of labor with land, for instance, helps to strengthen claims to that property against the claims of others. That mixing of labor is the extension of intentionality to objects, and helps create layers of individuality above those of such brute facts as mere spatio-temporal individuality. We value these intentional layers of individuality, and objects become transformed in culturally and socially important ways by human intentionality and its effects on individuation. Land becomes real-property, metal becomes an automobile, wedding cake becomes a memorial.

All objects in the world are individuals, but some objects are *more individual* than others, at least in that we value them differently. So what of human individuals? Does the same apply? It does, and human individuals attain different statuses due to the social nature of valuing.

Human Individuals, Persons, and Rights

Humans are individuals of a special sort. At the level of brute facts, each is an individual with a distinct spatio-temporal position and form. Each is also derived of and determined by a unique genome, which although it is very similar to the genomes of every other human being, differs from all others in important ways. These differences help determine the life-path of that human in significant ways, but environment plays an equally significant role, such as by causing even identical twins with identical genomes to diverge on distinct life-paths. The cultural and moral importance of distinct life-paths arises at the level of *personhood*. Persons are social constructs, existing above the level of the world of brute facts, superimposed on humans and possibly other types of organisms capable of certain states of affairs (like intentionality and reasoning). There are things that you cannot ethically do to human persons that you can do to mere human non-persons. Persons are the typical objects of most of our legal, social, and cultural norms. Persons have rights, duties, and obligations that human non-persons and other non-persons do not, although most humans are also persons for most of their lives. So far, *only* humans may at times be considered to be persons, and human individuality is part of the social construction of the person. Human individuality is necessary but insufficient for personhood.[13]

All of this is important because our decisions about using life-forms in various ways, including "owning" them through patents (e.g. plant patents and patents on genetically engineered life-forms), seem to relate in some way to the moral statuses of those life forms. Moral status is related to personhood. So we allow animal experimentation, and the creation of "knock-out" mice as animal models for diseases. Animal models must be killed after their use in an experiment is done, whereas human subjects of experiments must be cared for and never injured without some repercussions. Personhood informs our moral considerations, and to the extent that it relates to our genes, we should be wary of extending ownership claims over those things that help constitute this important status.

We are not going to develop a complete theory of personhood here. The task is ongoing and the subject of significant philosophical and legal discussion for some time. We must recognize, however, that personhood when it exists imports rights, duties and obligations. We have shown that it is thus far dependent upon the existence of human individuals (which is in-part dependent upon individual genetic make-up plus life-path), and that it is an object of social reality superimposed on the brute-fact object "humans." We must also recognize that the human genome plays an important role in personhood.

Personhood is present when certain mental states are present, including at least some necessary level of consciousness or developmental capacity to attain that level of consciousness. Other candidates for necessary mental states of personhood include: some decision-making capacity, some awareness of the world and ability to communicate that awareness, some minimum level of intelligence, some capacity to form and carry out intentions, etc. Each of these is determined in some part by genetics, as well as by environment and life-path. Humans lacking certain necessary genes will doubtless never achieve the mental states necessary for personhood. Thus personhood in humans is at least ontologically dependant on a human's genome. In other words, genes give us capacities that make us persons or not, and so personhood depends upon the presence or combination of certain genes within an organism, plus other factors that result in the cognitive states necessary for intentionality, reasoning, and the like. To the extent that all human persons share at least some minimum set of human genes necessary for personhood, the social object person is determined by some subset of brute facts. Our choices about which of those facts (for instance, which mental states) are required for personhood are socially construed. Indeed, looking historically at choices made by certain cultures at various times shows that many humans have at times been considered less than persons, and those choices now seem clearly unjust. Women, racial and ethnic groups, and mentally and physically disabled humans have at times been treated heinously due to the social construction of personhood at various historical periods.

Looking back at these abuses, it seems easy to criticize those choices as faulty by virtue of the brute facts of genetics. They were based on assumptions that were not borne out by the actual genetic make-up of those human persons who were left out from systems of justice that we can now criticize as inherently flawed. We know now that the genome reveals no significant differences among racial or ethnic groups, nor between men and women, nor for certain mental and physical disabilities. At least the genetic differences that have been revealed have not been at the level of those sorts of mental states necessary for personhood. In other words, historical attempts to cast women, racial and ethnic groups, and the disabled as less than persons were based upon faulty theories of mental capacities of each of those groups which are now contradicted by our present knowledge about the near-identity of each of those groups (except at the extreme fringes of certain disabilities) in their capacities.

Implications for Justice

If persons and genes are very tightly linked, then there would be reason to believe that patenting or otherwise owning genes would be more than a mere aberration in patent law. It might be an affront to individual liberty and equality. Some would have rights over parts of ourselves over which we as *possessors* of those parts have no particular rights. Such an unbalanced state of affairs would be both strange and repellent as we generally consider an aspect of autonomy to be control over parts of ourselves. Have we bargained away our autonomy unwittingly by granting others possession and control over parts of ourselves? Even setting aside issues of property or intellectual property law, these possibilities should raise ethical concerns. Privacy and autonomy are tightly linked, and even while we are bargaining away more of our privacy, often for the sake of security, we might wish to take a step back and consider whether we wish to do the same with parts of us so tightly linked to our conception of individuality, selfhood, and personhood.

Justice must at some level be based upon brute facts, even while legal systems are composed of social objects. We should take note that our investigation of human individuals and the social object "person" must depend on a scientific understanding of human individuals and their relations to their particular genomes as well as the human genome in general. Persons will always be the bearers of rights and objects of duties and obligations impacting our decisions about the extent to which ownership claims may be made against the human genome or particular human genomes. What we have revealed so far is some limit to our decisions, based on the onto-logical dependence of the relevant social objects on the world of brute facts. We have demonstrated a link between the genome, individual genomes, and the social object "person," and we have begun to reveal a connection between individuation and social norms of ownership. We have also revealed two levels of individuation: one at the level of brute facts, and one at the level of social objects. Now, let us consider the legal and social frame-work for the present regime of ownership of genes, both human and non-human, and see how they match up to the ontology so far revealed.

The law is the most important institution embodying notions of justice. It is important because unlike religions or private associations, which also may seek to embody and uphold justice, the law in its ideal form is insti-tuted among individuals at the level of the state and is applicable to every-one in a civil society. Laws and regulations already exist that govern the use of human tissues and property rights over their products. The laws have arisen both from legislatures and from courts, and have created sometimes conflicting rules about individual ownership over our bodies and the products of our tissues. These rules now cover genes extracted from tissue samples and now being housed and used in bio-banks. They conflict not only with each other, sometime granting individuals some control over their own tissues, and other times treating them as though they are fungi-ble, negotiable property in the hands of research scientists. These rules also seem to conflict with our intuitions about the realm of personal control we feel we have over ourselves and our bodies. Let's look at the law as it has developed and as it is currently applied to the ownership and alienability of human tissues and genes, and consider how these laws fit our intuitions, as well as whether they should be altered to conform with notions of justice.

5 | LEGAL DIMENSIONS IN GENE OWNERSHIP

The Role of the Law

The law is at the very least the public expression of currently held ethical and social norms through explicit prohibitions and requirements of behaviors. We tend to think of the law as reflecting more than mere desires or whims. In most traditions, the law is founded upon some extralegal view of morality. That is to say, legal prohibitions and punishments for murder are founded upon some moral prohibition that precedes the existence of the legal regime. Which does not imply that morality and the law overlap completely. There are many things that are morally repugnant that are nonetheless not legally prohibited. Lying, for instance, is generally not against the law (unless it's lying to the government, e.g. in court, or on your taxes). Failing to heed a stop sign is generally not considered immoral. But the law often represents a useful point of departure for investigating moral and ethical issues.

The law gives us some insight into those matters which a culture or society considers to be important, at least as represented through its legislature and courts. Laws are enacted where public interests are deemed vital enough to subject transgressors to punishment. Those interests that are considered most important tend to be covered by the criminal law, while other, lesser interests and rights are covered by the civil law. Often, the law protects what we consider to be "natural" rights (which I will argue later are really a priori rights). Natural rights have included, as stated explicitly by John Locke and adopted as slightly revised in the US Declaration of Independence, such things as "life, liberty, and property." Much of our criminal and civil law protects, to varying degrees, and with certain exceptions, each of these "natural" rights.

Because of the organic evolution of much of our law through the Anglo-Saxon common law and at various levels of federal and state government, sometimes legal concepts emerge that embody previously implicit rights that have never been fully worked out in public debate or through academic discourse. This is apparently what has happened in the realm of ownership of body parts and genes. The law, forced to grapple with an emerging new state of affairs for which no legislative solution had yet been developed, used older paradigms and precedents to forge a response. Part of that response was administrative on the part of a governmental agency (the Patent and Trademark Office (PTO)) faced with a new class of claim. Part of the response has also been through case law developed by courts.

Our law has, at various times, dealt with issues relating to the patenting of human tissues and products. The evolution of that law, and the reasoning behind it, together offer us some insight into the cultural, political, and ethical issues raised by schemes of ownership over human parts and products. That reasoning illuminates also the various objections or rationales behind the current state of the law of patenting genes. The present state of that law is a natural place to begin to grapple with some of the philosophical issues presented by DNA patents, as we will first explain the relevant case law before subjecting it to some serious criticism.

Autonomy and Property

We often use terms such as *liberty* and *autonomy* as though they are definite values, or in political discourse often as rights which are inviolable. Their entry into the Anglo-Saxon legal lexicon has been marked by some serious practical lapses. For instance, liberty interests, especially over one's own body, were not extended to large populations until well after the signing of the Declaration of Independence and the Constitution in the United States. Witness, for example, the existence of slavery prior to the Emancipation Proclamation and the 14th Amendment. Witness also the fact that women have, at various times, been treated as second-class citizens whose autonomy over their own bodies has been legally proscribed to various degrees, at various times, and in numerous cultures. It is strange that in this culture of *liberty*, where we seek to extend the notions of personal autonomy even beyond our borders by both diplomatic and somewhat less than diplomatic means, we have a very ill-defined notion of personal autonomy in one's body.

Simply put, under most legal systems you do not own your body as authoritatively or completely as you own, for instance, a tennis racket or car. You can smash your tennis racket if it fails you, or just for the heck of it. You can sell your car to anyone who can afford it, or even strip it down and sell it for scrap. Your property rights over moveables like these are nearly absolute. Your rights in certain chattels, like your herd of cattle, are also pretty nearly absolute. You can sell them for slaughter, or slaughter them yourself and auction off their parts. Strangely, you cannot do that with your own parts. You cannot market your kidney legally and you cannot generally choose to kill yourself. How is it that your property rights in your own body are restricted above and beyond your rights in, for instance, cattle? Moreover, are there any property interests that you could properly assert in the particular combination of the nearly three billion base pairs that comprise your DNA and give you, in large part, your individual identity and your basic attributes of personhood?

These are not merely academic questions. While it's unlikely that many people would start selling their kidneys were the practice to be legalized, a much greater potential violation of rights exists in the realm of intellectual property claims against the products of our bodies. Indeed, the courts have seemingly failed to keep up with the rapid growth of genetic technologies in the realm of pharmaceutics. They have refused to distinguish property rights in one's body parts from intellectual property rights in one's genes. Currently, there is a large gap in the jurisprudence which leaves unanswered fundamental questions about your rights in your body, your genes, and means of challenging those who may have already staked claims on the products of both. Let's look at this in light of developing case law, and consider some of the implications of what seems like a rather muddied area of jurisprudential philosophy.

Early Cases on Microorganisms and Animals: The Slope toward Human Patents

There are only a handful of cases prior to the 1970s that involved patenting non-human organisms. It was generally accepted at the time that naturally found organisms could not be patented. The Patent Commissioner at the time of the *Chakrabarty* (1980) decision, even noted "it was the general understanding . . . that legislation was needed if patent protection was to be extended to microorganisms."[1] *Chakrabarty* would change all that, at least by making the patenting of genetically-altered life-forms acceptable. Before this, however, such attempts almost universally failed. Let's look at some of those cases before examining *Chakrabarty* and its aftermath.

Up until *Chakrabarty*, hybridized or otherwise altered plants as well as similarly manipulated eggs, yeasts, and bacterial spores were afforded some patent protection. In each of these cases, the courts began to counter the assumption that no living thing could be patented (an assumption long acknowledged by the PTO) and looked rather at the novelty of the thing patented, whether living or dead, to determine whether it was properly considered an invention. Plants were patentable under a specific exception carved out of the Patent Act, first enacted in 1930 and then expanded in 1970, for hybridized plants developed through human intervention.[2] Microorganisms, and eventually higher animals, were at first considered problematic.

At the same time that Dr. Chakrabarty's application for a patent on his microbe was wending its way through the PTO, another microorganism patent was being considered and rejected. At Upjohn Research Laboratory, Michael Bergy had bred a strain of bacterium to manufacture the antibiotic lincomycin. Chakrabarty's microorganism was developed to digest petroleum. Both applications were originally rejected by their patent examiners as unpatentable "products of nature" under Section 101 of the Patent Act although in the case of Chakrabarty's microbe the examiner allowed the process patent for the process of creating the bacterium. The Patent Board overturned and rejected the entire patent in each case but not solely based on Section 101. Rather, the Board said that living organisms simply could not be patented.[3] The Board stated in *Bergy* that it had "extensively researched prior court decisions for guidance" on the issue of the patentability of living organisms but could find no case in point.[4] When *Bergy* and *Chakrabarty* went up on appeal, the Court of Patent Appeals rejected the notion that non-plant life-forms could not be patented, and they allowed the patents on these microorganisms because they could not otherwise be found in nature. These organisms were the products of human invention. The court looked at the little precedent that existed on patenting life, starting with the 1974 case *In re Mancy* which involved a method of cultivating an antibiotic by using a strain of *Streptomyces birfurcus*. The lower court had rejected the method as "obvious," citing the case *In re Kuel* and stating: "[h]ere appellants not only have no allowed claim to the novel strain of *Streptomyces* used in their process but would, we presume (without deciding), be unable to obtain such a claim because the strain, while new in the sense that it is not shown by any art of record, is, as we understand it, a 'product of nature.'"[5]

While some had interpreted *Mancy* as standing for the proposition that no life-form could be patented, this was explicitly rejected in *Bergy* where the appeals court stated: "we now make it explicit that the thought underlying our presumption that Mancy could not have obtained a claim to the strain of microorganism he had described was simply that it lacked novelty [but] our dictum was ill-considered."[6] In refining its position, the court looked at dictum from a Federal District Court in Delaware which had cast doubts on the patentability of life-forms. That case, *Guaranty Trust Co. of New York v. Union Solvents Corp.*[7] involved patent claims for a bacterial fermentation process in which the court allowed the patent for the process, but stated that if it were an application for a patent on the bacteria itself, then no patent would be allowed. The *Bergy* court summed up, stating "the fact that microorganisms, as distinguished from chemical compounds, are alive is a distinction without legal significance. . . ."[8] In *Chakrabarty*, the appeals court cited *Bergy* explicitly holding that the Patent Act is not limited to inanimate things and may apply to living inventions.[9] The path was now paved to patents on more complex organisms.

Patenting Animals

In 1987, the Patent Office had to grapple with the issue of patenting organisms larger than bacteria when considering the case *Ex parte Allen*. The patent involved a modified breed of oysters which were sterile and larger than usual. The examiner rejected the application because it involved a living creature, but the Patent Board overturned that reasoning based on *Chakrabarty* stating that the only relevant issue was whether the invention was created by man.[10] After this decision, the PTO released a policy statement which declared that all modified life-forms except for humans, were patentable subject matter, stating that it now "considers non-naturally occurring non-human muticellular living organisms, including animals, to be patentable subject matter . . . [but] [t]he grant of a limited, but exclusive property right in a human being is prohibited by the Constitution."[11] This prohibition was clearly a reference to the 13th Amendment's prohibition against slavery, but now the door had been opened wide to animal patents, for which applications had already been piling up.

The next year the first patent was granted for a multi-cellular organism. Harvard's famous "Harvard mouse" or "OncoMouse[TM]" was developed and patented as a model for human breast cancer studies.[12] Despite a flurry of lawsuits challenging the patent, often on moral or ethical grounds, the patent stands and thousands of animal patents have been successfully filed since 1988 on genetically modified creatures, although many companies held off for about five years expecting some sort of legislative action. Although there were hearings motivated often by religious concerns over genetic engineering in general, none of the 10 bills proposed ever emerged from the Congress explicitly banning genetic engineering of animals, or patents on life-forms.

At various times Congress expressed explicit concern over the slippery slope posed by animal patents toward a future of human patents. At a hearing, Congressman Robert Kastenmeier expressed doubts about the wisdom of *Chakrabarty*, and suggested that although the PTO had expressly forbidden patents on humans, some future administration might very well permit it.[13] A moratorium on patenting animals was proposed in the US Congress in August of 1987, but it was rejected in subcommittee.[14] The next year a nearly-identical bill was rejected by the Senate.[15] Similar measures were proposed and rejected or died in subcommittee. Behind most of these efforts were expressions of congressional concern that animal patents might lead to human patents, despite the PTO's express rejection of patenting humans based on the Constitution.

Several bills were eventually proposed by Senator Hatfield in the early 1990s, including a bill that would have imposed a two-year moratorium on not just animal patents, but also the patenting of "human tissues, fluids, cells, [and] genes or gene sequences." All of these proposed bills died in committee.[16] Meanwhile, cases dealing explicitly with patenting human tissues and products wound their way through the courts as Congress remained unable to provide any sort of legislative check.

Renting Your Spleen?

In a seminal case establishing the present state of the law regarding the genetic products of one's body, the Supreme Court of California considered a conversion claim, among others, in *John Moore v. The Regents of the University of Califonia.* 793 P.2d 479 (1990). Moore suffered from Hairy Cell Leukemia, and was undergoing treatments at the UCLA Medical Center. As part of the treatments he received, cells were extracted from him in ordinary testing procedures which included extracting bone marrow and blood. In the course of ordinary testing, the defendant physicians became aware that Moore's blood and bone marrow contained abnormalities that could be of significant scientific and commercial value. Moore made several claims in his complaint, but the one of most interest to us here was a claim for conversion – which means the unlawful use of another person's property for the enrichment of the person using the thing unlawfully. Defendants were interested in Moore's T-lymphocytes because they overproduced certain lymphokines. While lymphokines are produced by the identical gene in everyone, isolating Moore's cells was important to defendants in order to create a cell line that would benefit researchers in studying lymphokines in the future. The cell line produced from Moore's spleen cells was eventually patented by the defendants. The potential market for products relating to that patent was estimated to be roughly $3 billion US dollars. Defendants never intended to offer Moore royalties, believing that the consent forms he signed released them from any competing ownership interest in his tissues and its products. The court agreed, and declined to hold that there was any valid claim of conversion.

In *Moore*, after much discussion, probing several theories and counter-arguments to the notion of ownership over the products of one's own body, the court held: "[f]inally, the subject matter of the Regents' patent – the patented cell line and the products derived from it – cannot be Moore's property. This is because the patented cell line is both factually and legally distinct from the cells taken from Moore's body." While the court's reasoning is strained, and argues essentially that natural products can be patented if synthesizing them is sufficiently "difficult," the result in this particular case seems largely correct, at least regarding the conversion claim. There was nothing special about Moore's genes in the cell line, as the gene responsible for the production of lymphokines is identical in every human being. But two very important elements of this case with significant implications seem poorly considered and reasoned. Moreover, the reasoning from this case has deterred other courts from holding that people have divisible property interests in their own bodies and their products. Namely, the cells themselves may have ceased to be Moore's once excised, assuming proper consent to their being taken from him, but this does not *necessarily* imply either logically or legally that the *products* of those cells cease to be his, although the court quickly glosses over this point in the language quoted above. The court conflates interests in tokens with interests in types, which is part of the slippery slope that leads us to the present problem of gene patents.

Take the following counter-examples: a model signs a release for use of his likeness in a photo-shoot aimed only at demonstrating the photographer's skill. The photographs of the model certainly are the property of the photographer, but if the photographer were to sell those images for use in an advertising campaign for, let's say, toothpaste, then the model would have a claim for misappropriation of his likeness. Or suppose that I am an author of a book and there's only one copy of it in the world. I sell the book, and the buyer decides she could make money by copying the book and selling the copies. This too would be a misappropriation, although she was lawfully in possession of the only original copy of that book. One's likeness and the products of one's creativity are treated as sorts of property, misappropriations of which are subject to punishment and remuneration. Why then are the products of one's own body, and even perhaps one's own unique genes, not entitled to the status of a form of personal property whose alienation (sale or donation for use) must be specifically consented to, and which ought to be properly remunerated when that use profits someone else? The *Moore* case sets the precedent that no benefits need to accrue to the original donor.

The Move to Human Gene Patents

With no explicit administrative nor legislative prohibition against patenting human tissues or products of humans (as opposed to humans themselves) and with frantic work conducted and completed on mapping the human genome from the late 1990s to the present time, gene patents have exploded. Craig Venter's Celera Corp. justified its massive expenditures on gene sequencing technologies by beginning the practice of filing raw gene patents in the 1990s using *Moore* and *Chakrabarty* to justify its applications. Now, according to the PTO, genes and gene fragments are considered patentable subject matter. In its Utility Examination Guidelines published January 5, 2001, the PTO notes that "patenting compositions or compounds isolated from nature follows well-established principles, and is not a new practice," and cites US Patent 141,072 filed in 1873 by Louis Pasteur for a yeast as an "article of manufacture," as well as a synthesized form of human adrenaline.[17] The reasoning offered is that the patent does not cover the gene itself as it occurs in nature, but only its isolated or purified form which is considered a new composition of matter. Under the Patent Act, a composition of matter must be novel, useful, and non-obvious to be patentable. But isolating and synthesizing a naturally-occurring compound ordinarily only results in a patent for the process involved, not for the compound itself. The Pasteur patent was a blatant exception to the general rule, and the only such patent until the twentieth century, and the adrenaline patent covered the *process* of extraction, not adrenaline itself which occurs naturally in many organisms.

It was on the basis of *Moore* and the *Chakrabarty* decision (allowing for patenting of altered genetic products), that Celera Corp. began filing patents on the products of their private investment in the Human Genome Project (HGP) race in the mid-1990s. Celera's attorney began hastily filing patent claims on wild-type genes discovered by their sequencing and annotation of the human genome, reasoning that *Chakrabarty* and *Moore* served as precedent for the patenting of even unaltered human genetic products.[18] Of course, the donors to Celera gave consent knowing that Celera was, in fact, using their genomes to develop a map of the human genome. Perhaps they did not know that, along the way, Celera and other companies would begin to stake out broad swaths of the territory of that map and claim them as their own.

The PTO has since clarified and refined the various requirements for patenting genes. Non-obviousness is met so long as the gene or gene sequence has not yet been described as a composition of matter before the patent application. A patent must also enable one skilled in the relevant field to replicate the invention, and that requirement is considered met by gene patents where one can read the gene sequence and thus locate it. The utility requirement was made a bit more stringent in January 2001 after complaints that too many gene patents were issuing. The new guidelines establish two tests for utility, only one of which has to be met. The first is the "specific, substantial, and credible utility test" which requires specificity over the part of the gene claimed, "substantial utility" via some real-world use of the patented sequence, and credibility via some demonstration that the patented sequence is "currently available for such use."[19]

Human DNA patents now issue for structures, functions, and processes of genes, and all are considered compositions of matter. Typically, however, the uses of these patents are suspect, and ought to give us pause. Consider the use of a gene sequence in nature, as opposed to the uses for which we are currently able to put genes. In nature, genes direct cell development and metabolism. However, typical human gene patents specify the use as screening for that particular gene. Of course, there are expected (but generally unknown or un-perfected at the time of filing) downstream uses of the genes. Take, for example, Patent 7,326,781, "polynucleotides encoding the human citron kinase polypeptide, BMSNKC.sub.-0020/0021." This is a gene patent on a segment of the human genome. It's easy to look this up at www.uspto.gov. Just search for that patent number and try reading through it. It contains numerous claims, including several statements about its supposed novelty. Of course, the novelty requirement is easily met because gene patents now need only encompass new *discoveries* of human genes (rather than inventions) and the utility requirements include several potential uses for the gene, for instance, in creating monoclonal antibodies, through recombinant DNA techniques, or in developing screening tests for the specified gene. In essence, this patent covers a segment of human DNA (specifically a gene) that directs the production of a certain antibody. While the gene is clearly *useful* to human bodies and might be put to use for the synthesis of antibodies, it is clearly a product of nature. The only thing the inventor has done is to point out, as if on a map, where that gene lies in nature. They have also successfully isolated that gene in order to get the patent, just like proceeding from a land survey and then marking out physically the boundaries of a certain piece of land. So where's the real invention? The atmosphere is clearly *useful* in filtering out dangerous radiation so that we all can live, but no one could patent the sky.

To isolate their gene and apply for their patent, the "inventors" have only employed well-established techniques of human genome "map-reading" and used off-the-shelf technologies for isolating segments of that map and reproducing them. It is a bit like using Global Positioning Systems (GPS) technology to define the borders of some previously unexplored landmark and then seeking intellectual property protection on the landmark itself claiming that the GPS coordinates delineating the landmark set it apart from the landmark "in its natural state" and thus make it suddenly patentable. In the process, new roadblocks have clearly emerged for all who would wish to survey that property themselves. Although the PTO has claimed that gene patents do not encompass genes in their natural state, they do just that for all intents and purposes. We might feel a bit relieved to know that when we reproduce we aren't violating anyone's patent, but any scientist wishing to explore scientifically that gene sequence does so at his or her own risk because it is now legally bounded territory. It is off-limits unless you wish to pay a toll to explore that section of the roadmap of human DNA. Things get even stranger when we begin to consider that some people now *own* diseases.

Patenting Diseases

The Federal District Court of the Southern District of Florida recently grappled with part of the aftermath of this unprecedented land-grab in a case involving a patent on the gene responsible for Canavan's disease. In *Greenberg v. Miami Children's Hospital Research Institute, Inc.*, 264 F.Supp.2d 1064 (S.D. Fl. 2003), Greenberg was one of several donor plaintiffs who gave tissue samples with the understanding that defendants would use them to develop a cure for the disease, and that the information developed through the research would remain in the public domain. Defendants actually filed and obtained a patent for the gene itself. In 1994, defendants acquired Patent No. 5,679,635, which described the gene for Canavan's disease, foreclosing other researchers from studying the disease without infringing the patent unless they paid license fees. The patent issued in 1997, and plaintiffs learned of it in 1998. The plaintiffs were some of those people who had donated the tissue that helped the researchers to discover the gene responsible for the disease. They sued claiming, among other things, conversion.

While recognizing that "[u]sing property given for one purpose for another purpose constitutes conversion [citation omitted]," the court held that "[p]laintiffs have no cognizable property interest in body tissue and genetic matter donated for research under a theory of conversion," citing *Moore* as authority. Once again, the court held that the property rights in the tissue, and the *information* contained in that tissue, were somehow indivisible. In other words, they were treated as one in the same, with one property interest flowing from the other. Since this case, and following the vast land-grab by Celera and numerous other corporations and universities, nearly 20 percent of the human genome has been patented. Still, the courts treat the tissue and the genes in it simultaneously as alienable property. You bargain both away at once, wittingly or unwittingly – donor beware. There seems to be a logical disconnect in this approach given that the courts have, 1 decided to apply intellectual property law to natural genetic products, and 2 the laws of privacy and torts give special status to individual identity and bodily autonomy in other contexts. Let's examine

the most recent case involving these issues before considering the implications and alternatives.

Consider the practical effect of the Canavan's disease example: there are
thousands of people suffering from this disease, and now anyone searching
for a cure must tread carefully. It is a genetic disease. It is monogenic,
meaning that everyone with that particular gene has the disease or is a
carrier. To do research on developing potential new genetic treatments for
the disease, one must necessarily consider the economics of paying royalties
to the patent-holder, or risk litigation if one doesn't. Or perhaps there are
researchers out there who go to their labs every day expecting to do science
and not to do patent searches before they tackle an important or challenging problem. Scientists and drug companies function differently after all.
Scientists often do work on matters for which they expect no particular
commercial or technological result. Now scientists must concern themselves with potential infringement claims if their science leads them into
one of the growing number of claimed territories in the human genome,
or even the genomes of their lab animals. Animals, as we have seen, share
much of our DNA, so it's entirely conceivable that patented human gene
sequences exist in the same forms in countless other creatures. So what's a
scientist to do to avoid a suit?

Catalona and Beyond

In *Washington University v. Catalona* 437 F. Supp. 2d 985 (E.D. Missouri
2006), a physician (Catalona) had meticulously collected prostate cell
samples for decades, resulting in a cell library of nearly 30,000 samples. He
did this while affiliated with the plaintiff Washington University. Eventually,
the defendant physician left Washington University for a new position and
sought to take his library of samples. Washington University insisted the
samples were the property of the university and not of Catalona personally.
Although Catalona sought and received the consent of nearly 6,000
of the original donors to take the samples with him, the court held that
the samples were the property of Washington University, and that the donors
retained no rights to further direct their samples be sent with Catalona.

The court noted:

> WU's Intellectual Property Policy states that "all intellectual property
> (including . . . tangible research property) shall be owned by the University

if significant University resources were used or if it is created pursuant to a research project funded through corporate, federal, or other external sponsors administered by the University." Plaintiff's Exhibit 17, ß I..3(a). It further states "[G]enerally, creators and research investigators will retain custody of tangible research property while at the University." 437 F.Supp. 987–88.

It then considered the question of the proper ownership of the samples, once again treating the property rights not as divisible interests, but rather treating the tissues and the information encoded within them as one in the same, and applying the law of gifts and property:

> Missouri law governs the substantive issues of ownership and "gift/ donation". It is well-settled that exclusive possession and control of personal property is prima facie evidence of ownership, and anyone else claiming such property bears the burden of proof. 437 F.Supp. 992

Applying the reasoning from both *Moore* and *Greenberg*, the *Catalona* court reasoned simultaneously that donors retain no property interest in their tissues (much less the information encoded in them), and that the university which received the sample received an *inter vivos* gift which it essentially holds in "fee simple absolute," against all other claims of title, present intent of the donors be damned. The upshot is that recipients of tissue donations have stronger legal property interests in those tissues than each of us has in our own present tissues or body. At the very least, however, *Catalona* recognizes that body parts can be property, presenting an opening for future arguments regarding present possession, control, profits, and conscious alienation.

Gene patents issued in the wake of all these decisions present a number of potential profit streams or sources of value for those who extract tissues, while the system still offers nothing for the donors of the tissue from which the products are derived. Gene patents often cover not just the gene, but also the protein product of the gene as well as other isolated gene fragments within the gene. Typically the claims are vague about what potential uses might come from these genes, products or fragments. While property rights are being granted to the "inventors" (who are really just discoverers) of these elements of individual human bodies and generally the whole species, no one has expressed any limiting property claims either by the donors of the tissues, nor of the species itself that possesses these genes in common.

It seems odd that, on the one hand, property rights are readily applied to collections of samples, the value of which is not so much in their forms as tokens (the individual cells in the samples) but rather in the information they encode, which could be garnered from other sets and other samples but for the time and cost of collection. But the most potentially valuable part, the *information* in those samples, is treated during the collection as something indivisible from the cells themselves, as easily bargained away as the physical cells, yet capable of producing enormous profits in the hands of biotech companies. These cases begin to illustrate the confusion faced not just by the courts, nor simply by the PTO or Congress, but even by the researchers themselves who are now apparently conflating monetary value (via bio-banks or genetic databanks) with scientific value which may or may not inhere in any collection of human cells.

What's so Strange about the Law of Bodies and Tissues?

Simply put, the law is being applied oddly in that:

1 products of nature are being patented for the first time (witness the gene for Canavan's disease);
2 while the law of intellectual property treats property rights as divisible (so that one can, for instance, sell or buy a book without simultaneously transferring rights to the information *in* the book), it is not treating one's rights to one's own DNA similarly, even while applying intellectual property law as a paradigm for DNA products;
3 as a consequence, individuals have greater rights in their likenesses, and to privacy of their medical records than over the commercialization of their genetic identities.

While we speak often about autonomy and liberty, there is no legal guarantee of integrity over either our bodies (for there are certain things the law directs that we may not do with our own bodies, such as ingest certain harmful substances, sell our kidneys, or kill ourselves), or over our genetic identities. If there is anything that modern genetic science and technology teaches us, it is that DNA is an utterly unique product of nature, directing its own reproduction and evolution in the remarkable diversity of life in nearly every environment on earth. Not only is DNA unique, but its forms are many and varied, even while its building blocks are simple and may be found in similar forms across diverse species. The fruit fly, for instance, shares numerous genes serving similar purposes with many other creatures including humans. Genes responsible for certain traits in mice serve similar or identical purposes in other mammals including humans. Similarities among closely related species are even more striking, with chimps and humans sharing 96 percent of the same genetic code. Similarities within species are even more pronounced, with each one of us as humans sharing 99+ percent of the same genetic material. And yet, we have important differences that mark our individual genetic identities, as unique and distinguishing as fingerprints or our likenesses. These facts present us with important reasons to question the present state of the law of ownership of human body parts, tissues, and genetic products. These questions include:

1   Is intellectual property law a workable paradigm for ownership of genes when DNA is a product of natural evolution and not of ingenuity or inventiveness?
2   Is the human genome the property of any one individual, or of the species itself, given its role in producing our species' genetic identity and given its similarities with other species?
3   Are our individual genetic identities, given their roles in creating us as unique individuals, distinct even in important ways from others within our species, and are they our personal property in ways in which even our tissues may not be?

These questions have not been answered adequately in the case law so far, and courts have not grappled sufficiently with the ethical implications involved in allowing for private ownership of naturally occurring genes and their products possessed by humankind as a whole.

The Law of Personal Identity

Even though the law recognizes little in the way of property or privacy rights over your body or its products once they leave your body, it does recognize protection for other parts of you, such as your image or other indicia of your identity. This was, in fact, a line of argument in *Moore* that was utterly ignored – analogizing the law of privacy and identity to rights in body parts and products. The law has recognized for some time that others ought not to profit from the unlicensed use of one's image or personality in most contexts. The common law first recognized that individuals have privacy rights in the use of their images, at least where the use is commercial or profitable. A number of states specifically create privacy rights for individuals over the use of their images for advertising purposes, and courts have recognized the same rights long before statutes were passed. The individual right has been applied to both uses in "trade" and more specifically for "advertising." Incidental references or minor uses will not ordinarily suffice to infringe one's right to one's identity or image, and the use must be specifically linked to the person's "value" in such a way as to profit from the person's identity. Consent to have one's image used invalidates any claim, but consent must typically be made in writing. Consent may be broad or narrow. A general waiver allows for using the image, likeness or other visible identity in any way one pleases (except in some cases for "immoral" purposes), but consent may also be narrowly tailored for specific purposes.[20]

Public figures are typically deemed to waive their rights of privacy, but even a public personage may sue one who seeks to exploit that person's fame for his or her own benefit, unless of course they have specifically consented. An individual's right of privacy may be invaded by the use of his or her name or likeness, without consent, to imply his or her endorsement of a product, or by appropriating his or her name for promotional purposes, as by using it to identify a product, or by using other means to identify one with another's business. It may also be invaded by misrepresenting his or her authorship of something published.

People may have causes of action (a right to sue) where their pictures are altered or used in error, or where their names or pictures are used primarily to increase the circulation of a publication. The law has allowed plaintiffs recovery for unauthorized uses of images of individuals in newspapers, motion pictures, and television. Thirty-five states in the US now recognize this right of privacy, but there is no federal statutory provision. Some states like California require a showing of injury in order to recover for commercial misappropriation of one's image, while others require no such showing. Interestingly, the law seems to have carved out a right of privacy over the commercial use of our images that is stronger than any right anyone has over the use of our genes. One might argue that a blanket waiver over the use of one's tissue is the same as the blanket waiver over the use of one's image. Most savvy attorneys, however, know to limit the scope of the consent used for those taking people's images, whereas most people whose tissue is being extracted do not have the benefit of the advice of an attorney. Moreover, the future uses of images are limited necessarily given the limited natural uses to which images may be put, but tissue samples that received blanket waivers prior to genetic sequencing technologies may now be mined for uses for which the donors could have had no prior expectation of possible use.

Reconciling the Law with Reality

The move from patenting hybridized plants, to genetically-altered micro-organisms, to human tissues and genes, has been the epitome of the fabled slippery slope. While some have raised questions and even attempted to slow or stop the process with legislative roadblocks, they have proven to be unsuccessful. There are clearly those in the marketplace who have staked much on the value of human gene patents. As detailed in the story of Celera's involvement with mapping the human genome, staking claims to genes was essentially the greatest value statement that appeased Celera's stockholders in that expensive data venture. Had the human genome remained in the public domain, as it was bound to had it been wholly completed by the international HGP, we would not find ourselves in the present situation. Arguably, it would have taken much longer to complete the HGP, since Celera's expanding patent portfolio and stock price helped spur the project forward faster. But there are significant issues raised now by the current conundrum, where much of the human genome is now being claimed under patents, as well as diseases and other parts of other genomes in the varieties of life-forms on the planet. Among these issues are those for which the legal system, both through courts and legislatures, may have been ill-equipped to appropriately resolve complex scientific or philosophical problems of identity and ownership. Sometimes, the law is slow to catch up to significant economic, cultural, social, or practical considerations. This does not mean it's too late to catch up, nor does it require acceptance of something that we only discover later is substantially wrong. Legal institutions are meant to regulate human behaviors, to benefit the public good, and to ensure order and predictability.

The law often corrects itself. The history of jurisprudence is rife with examples of 180 degree turns in the face of injustices. Courts and legislatures sometimes change their minds. Witness, for instance, sharp turns on slavery, on segregation, on women's rights, and other major milestones in the evolution of civil rights and liberties both in the US and worldwide. In intellectual property law, the most rapid and influential changes have occurred in US law given its role in international technological and scientific innovation, and the wide reach of US patent and trademark law through treaties such as the World Intellectual Property Organization (WIPO). On the issue of patenting genes, surprisingly and boldly, other nations have balked. European law has refused to grant the sorts of wide protections to human gene patents claimed by US inventors. It may well be time for American courts and legislators to revisit these laws yet again, provide some consistency and clarity, and bring the law back in line with some notions of justice. One good reason (as we shall see later) is purely economic, given that gene patents impact our ability to innovate. We'll discuss more fully later how gene patents are a very real burden on the scientific enterprise, and how US science might well suffer as a result. There is also a clear disconnect between US patent law as applied to genes, and international agreements, including one devised by the United Nations Educational, Scientific, and Cultural Organization (UNESCO), which has issued a "Universal Declaration on the Human Genome and Human Rights" (1997). That declaration explicitly forbids individual profit in Article 4, stating: "The human genome in its natural state shall not give rise to financial gains."

There is clearly a gap between our intuitions about the relations between our individual genomes, our identities, perceptions of privacy and personal autonomy, and the law. Moreover, the courts seem to have contradicted themselves in simultaneously applying intellectual property law to naturally occurring genes and genetic products, and yet failing to treat donors' rights to their body parts and products as divisible from any rights to the information inherent in those parts and products. Finally, we may wish to reconsider the nature of DNA and genes in light of the science, and consider them as unique products, to which old paradigms might not apply. Perhaps naturally occurring genes and their products are forms of commons that cannot be enclosed, and which are part of a larger common heritage best left in the public domain? We have rushed headlong into the present situation with little thought of these rather metaphysical, but essential issues. We should face them now and clear up this muddied area of law, technology, and ethics.

6 | ARE GENES INTELLECTUAL PROPERTY?

The law has so far treated genes as a form of intellectual property. Specifically, genes are treated as patentable. The Patent Act, as it has been interpreted in the US enables the first inventor to successfully file a patent to exclude others from making or selling his or her new, useful, and non-obvious invention or improvement upon an existing invention. Because of various treaty organizations and agreements, US patents have been applied outside of the US, including patents over genes. Patents protect processes, methods, manufactures, and compositions of matter. Patents do not protect ideas, but rather exclude the use of those ideas by others. Patent protection has been extended to genes and gene segments, as well as to the products and processes associated with both. Patent applications typically state numerous claims, some or all of which might be granted, or separately struck down by the Patent and Trademark Office (PTO) as falling outside the scope of patent protection. By now, many thousands of gene patents have been granted, and included among the claims of most of these are the representations of the gene sequences themselves, meaning the string of bases depicted by the letters A, C, T and G. Are genes properly protected under patent, or under any other existing intellectual property scheme?

We arrived at this place without much in the way of reasoned introspection, and the courts and PTO have at times reasoned along similar, or at times divergent, paths. The legislature has more or less sat out the debate, with only modest attempts at various times to weigh in on the patentability of genes. So it has been up to the courts, and the PTO, each supposedly guided by the Constitutional grant of Congress's authority to create the patent system for the purposes of encouraging the creative and useful arts. Clearly, gene patents are perceived as very useful. They are certainly valuable, and they are part of the patent portfolios of many universities and pharmaceutical companies. There are now many entrenched interested parties ready to lobby for the status quo, but there are also those who have come out vocally opposed to gene patents, often on ethical, moral, or religious grounds. Legal theorists and intellectual property scholars have similarly weighed in on the patentability of genes. We should consider this question, separate and apart from the moral and ethical considerations of gene patents, and ask for now whether under any theory of intellectual property genes may properly be considered capable of protection.

First, let's consider the question of what qualifies as intellectual property, and under what conditions? This question requires a bit of review, including both the philosophical justifications of intellectual property and the historical antecedents to this rather new form of property protection. Once we look at the nature of intellectual property in its various forms, we can ask whether genes have the necessary and sufficient features for belonging to the category of objects capable of receiving intellectual property protection, which particular intellectual property categories they might belong to, and whether they are capable or worthy of other forms of protection.

The Historical Development of Intellectual Property

Ideas are unbounded and uncontainable. The only way to protect them from use by others is by secret-keeping. In fact, secret-keeping was the first form of intellectual property protection, and still accounts for an economically significant amount of protection for various "trade-secrets," such as the formula for Coca-Cola™ or Kentucky Fried Chicken,™ as well as thousands of industrial and commercial products and processes. But trade secrets do not prevent independent discovery and use, and offer no recourse if someone else happens upon your secret all on their own. The adage goes that "ideas want to be free" and refers to the unmitigated fact that ideas, once expressed, cannot be contained and can flow freely absent any regulatory framework from one thinker to another. Any intentionally-produced man-made object is an expression of ideas. This includes both objects that last over time and those that are ephemeral. A statue is an expression, as is a printing press or a computer. Verbal statements are expressions and so are physical signs and hand signals. There are distinctions among expressions which are both practically and theoretically important, and which have warranted differing forms of legal protections under various intellectual property schemes. Expressions that last over time (in some "fixed" state) are the only ones generally afforded intellectual property protection, while legal regimes almost universally recognize that expressions that are ephemeral (like unrecorded verbal statements or gestures) cannot be protected. Moreover, ideas cannot legally be protected at all unless they are somehow expressed, and then only by certain institutional means within the positive legal systems we have created.

Once an idea is expressed it becomes easily copied. Often ideas are valuable separate and apart from their expressions. Take, for instance, manmade fire. The fire can certainly be utilized and enjoyed by a whole community without anyone but the fire-starter knowing or understanding how it was ignited. The fire-starter may keep the secret of fire-making from all and maintain his or her status by doing so. The secret may be kept from everyone, although there is no way to prevent some sort of independent discovery. Others may well discover methods of starting fires, but if the fire-starter shares his or her fire with others at a reasonable cost (perhaps a modest share of the hunt) then others may simply weigh the relative cost of trading for ready-made fire versus the cost of a research program aimed at independent discovery. Moreover, should others discover independently the means of making fire, it may well profit both discoverers to agree to keep the secret to ensure a market for their services, protecting each through a contract not to divulge their methods. This is the way guilds operate.

When the printing press was first invented, it was well beyond the means of most people to reverse engineer and manufacture their own, and the methods of manufacturing and using a printing press could be kept secret. Printing guilds ensured that even while the products of the printing press involved knowledge which could be marketed (such as leaflets, flyers, and books), knowledge of the *manner* by which books and leaflets were made was kept closely held by a select group of craftsmen who agreed to secrecy to preserve their market share and prices. Secret-keeping was often enforced by the use of actual force if others learned of the trade secrets involved in a process but refused to become part of the guild. It is clear that historically speaking, secret-keeping is the precursor to all others forms of intellectual property protection. Now, however, it remains a rather risky form of protecting one's intellectual property as the guild system no longer exists, and anti-monopoly laws would make the tactics of guilds unenforceable as illegal. Independent discovery can always undermine a secret, and modern technology makes reverse-engineering most inventions easier than ever. As printing presses proliferated and technology improved, secret-keeping became impractical as a means of protecting many ideas from use by others. Both inventions and primarily aesthetic expressions were capable of reproduction by others, and new means of institutionalized protections were necessary.[1]

In the early fifteenth century the first robust institutionalized forms of intellectual property protection emerged in Europe. Renaissance Italy and Britain each developed separately rudimentary patent systems designed to encourage innovators to either import themselves, their works of authorship, or inventions to the benefit of local and national economies. In England, "letters patent" were issued directly by the monarch to inventors from abroad who agreed to settle in Britain to practice and produce their craft or invention. A "letter patent" from the sovereign gave the inventor who received it the exclusive right to market his or her product for a term of years. After concerns about the abuse of patents, and unreasonably long terms or indefinite renewals, the Statute of Monopolies was passed by the Parliament in 1623 to limit the term of patents.[2] The colonies employed similar patent provisions and when the US Constitution was being debated, the Founders included Article 1, Section 8, which is a specific constitutional grant of authority for Congress to regulate patents and copyrights for inventors and authors. Pursuant to its constitutional authority, The US Congress instituted the Patent Commission in 1790. The PTO now presides over patents and copyrights in the US, while numerous other similar legal institutions exist throughout other nations. There are also internationally recognized treaty organizations protecting patents internationally.[3]

Historically speaking, intellectual property regimes are relatively new. Unlike common law schemes which long protected property rights over goods, chattels, and land, state-sanctioned monopolies over works of authorship and inventions have developed through specific legal enactments intended to encourage innovation in the arts and technical sciences. In the past 50 years, intellectual property laws have changed considerably in the US, lengthening the time periods of protection now to the lifetime of the author plus 75 years in the case of copyrights, and 20 years from filing for patents. Intellectual property law has, since its inception, always included some tradeoff between the interests of authors and inventors on the one hand, and the interests of the public on the other. The balance of the interests has been moving recently toward strengthening the rights of authors and inventors, and keeping intellectual property out of the public domain for longer periods of time. Recent revisions in the law have strengthened the state-sanctioned monopoly presumably to provide even greater incentives for innovation. At the same time, intellectual property has become a significant asset in corporate holdings, often outweighing so-called "bricks and mortar" holdings in relative value to the share price. Companies like Microsoft and Google are valued not for their "tangible" assets, so much as for their "intangible" or intellectual property holdings. Patents and copyrights now figure prominently in corporate balance sheets as assets affecting the market valuation of all sorts of companies, and serve as steady and predictable sources of revenue flow over long periods of time.

DNA and gene patents held by pharmaceutical companies, often farmed out through technology transfer offices from university research labs, are a new and potentially profitable addition to corporate patent portfolios. But are they even properly considered to be intellectual property? Let's examine the theory of intellectual property implicit in its historical development, and then look more closely at the question of whether genes belong to the general category "intellectual property."

The Theory of Intellectual Property

Because it is the nature of ideas that they are easily copied and difficult to contain, positive (man-made) laws are considered necessary to create greater incentives for authors and inventors to produce things of value. Unlike other types of property, the value of intellectual property is not in the tokens (each individual instance) but rather in the types. That is to say, the control that is given by intellectual property is not over the individual instances of the inventions or books on the market or possessed by others. Anyone may purchase these instances, give them away, destroy, or resell them. Yet traveling with each instance or token is still some limitation: the right to exclude *certain* uses to which the owner of each instance might wish to put the tokens in their possession. Ordinary property is not like this. If a book or an invention is in the public domain (or historically speaking, prior to any intellectual property law), the owner of any instance may make copies, thus exerting some control not just over the token, but over the type. States began to develop the notion of intellectual property not to grant rights to inventors, but rather to limit the rights of others to produce and profit from works of authorship or inventions of others for a period of time. The notion behind this is that authors and inventors will have a greater incentive to produce works of authorship or to invent useful items and introduce them into the stream of commerce if they can assure themselves a certain share of the profits of every copy sold for a certain period of time before those rights revert back into the public domain.

Because of the fluidity and ease of use of ideas, once they are out there in the world expressed in either an aesthetic or a utilitarian work, some positive scheme of institutionalized protection is necessary to provide an incentive to express ideas in the first place. Guilds or private licenses or contracts do not bear the weight of a state-sanctioned monopoly, and therefore states provide the market leverage needed to enforce the bargain. Civil and criminal sanctions back up the laws, and there are a number of tradeoffs made by both the author or inventor and the public.

Some historians and philosophers of intellectual property also point out a Lockean justification for intellectual property rights. This school of thought justifies granting rights to authors and inventors not merely as a utilitarian tool to encourage the aesthetic and useful arts, but rather out of a moral argument for rewarding *intellectual* labor with ownership.[4] Just as the mixing of labor with land gives moral justification for ownership of land to those who improve it (in the Lockean perspective), so granting the right of profit to those who mix their intellectual labor with other materials is similarly morally justified.[5] Whatever the theoretical justification, there are a number of practical trade-offs and concerns built into any legal scheme of intellectual property protection intended to serve the dual purposes of providing incentives for authorship and invention, and ensuring that the public ultimately benefits by increased access to knowledge.

One tradeoff for inventors is that their inventions not only lapse back into the public domain after a period of time, but upon receiving a patent, the entire scheme of methods, processes, and manufacture of their inventions are disclosed. Anyone may review a patent that has been granted and understand fully how it works because the law requires that level of disclosure, and we may all therefore improve our understanding of the science and technology involved. By replacing secret-keeping with full disclosure, knowledge is moved more quickly into full public view and more innovation is potentially spurred. No patent holder may ever claim monopoly over the *ideas* behind the patent. The same is true for works of authorship. In intellectual property law, this is known as the "idea/expression dichotomy." Intellectual property limits the expression of ideas, either via utilitarian works (such as patentable products or processes) or aesthetic works (the subject of copyright) and yet the law never forbids the knowledge of an *idea*. Ideas remain always in the public domain. Intellectual property laws are created out of the recognition that ideas themselves cannot be protected and that secret-keeping is often ineffective or counterproductive to the public good. The state (the public) therefore limits the use of tokens, preventing their reproduction without royalties to the author or inventor for some fixed term so that authors freely release their works to the public. All of this theoretically results in increasing the public knowledge base, spurring more innovation, and rewarding authors for their investments in their works.

Because intellectual property law is meant to encourage innovation, and because it does not protect bare ideas but rather their expressions, there are certain inherent limitations on the subjects of legal protection. Only expressions may be prevented from unauthorized reproduction, but one natural limit is that the expression must itself be somehow "fixed" in some medium. Thus, singing a song one has heard on the radio does not violate the author's copyright, but recording that song and offering it for sale does. The patent on an invention is not violated by taking the thing apart, nor by reverse engineering in order to fully understand the product or process, but only by creating a physical copy. A lecture about the product or process does not violate the patent. Each individual expression, each token of the item, whether it is a book, film, pill, or machine, may be sold without royalties to the inventor after the first sale. So when you liquidate your library, or sell your flat-screen TV, no further royalties go to the copyright holder or inventor. This is known as the "first sale" doctrine. Anything else would clearly be unmanageable as tracking the string of royalties owed would inhibit trade in anything used.

Copyright and patents cannot protect ideas, so there are certain limits to the extent of protection afforded and the patentability or copyrightability of anything that is too close to being an idea rather than a particular expression of that idea. The idea of an obsessed sea captain's hunt for an elusive white whale would not be copyrightable, whereas Melville's particular string of words, story elements, and characters are protectable (or were until the copyright expired) under copyright law. The idea of using gravity to lift people from one floor to another is not patentable, but the means by which Otis™ reduces this idea to practice is patentable, but only to the extent that they used novel techniques and technology that were non-obvious to one skilled in the art. Laws of nature are not patentable. Their particular uses in new, useful, and non-obvious inventions are patentable. Laws of nature that are not currently known, but that later become discovered through science, are not patentable. This is an important exemption for the purposes of our discussion of genes. It is clear, however, that laws of nature do not fit the usual requirements for intellectual property protection. They are not novel, although they may be put to novel uses. The laws of nature are inherent in the universe – they exist despite our knowledge. Intellectual property law is meant to encourage invention and innovation in the aesthetic and useful arts. The law is not meant to encourage mere discovery.

Discovery is often extremely useful, but it is the province of science not of technology. Discovery often precedes and enables technology, but not every new discovery leads to a patentable new technology. Science should be free to explore nature without fear of treading on intellectual property rights. Science might inform technology, but the two are distinct in their objects, methods, and means of support. Science has traditionally been funded by states, through universities or research centers, and not through profits from inventions. Only recently have intellectual property rights emerged as potential rewards for scientists pursuing pure research at their universities.[6] This recent development, as we shall see, has blurred the traditional roles and distinctions between pure research and technological innovation, and this complication weighs heavily in the current debate over the patentability of genes. The important qualification that has always existed, that discoveries and laws of nature are not patentable (only inventions are), is what has maintained a delicate balance and respectful distance between researchers delving into nature's secrets and technologists employing their discoveries in new and useful inventions.

Imagine if laws of nature or discoveries were protected. Einstein could have patented relativity, preventing its use without paying him royalties for every nuclear reactor or atom bomb. Albeit, he might have taken his science a step further and dreamed up a technology (like nuclear reactors or atom bombs) and patented those. Patenting the discovered parts of nature, the laws themselves, grants too broad of a right that is potentially prohibitive and which rewards something that the law of intellectual property was never meant to protect. Laws of nature are not the result of human invention or innovation, and thus those who discover them are not given any incentive to produce anything useful. One could profit by mere discovery, without having to put the discovery to any useful technology. One could devise, for instance, a full explanation of why things fall toward each other and then patent the law of gravity, without having to put it to any publicly useful purpose. Then one could sue Otis™, or whoever else comes along with a new invention employing gravity, and then demand royalties. Clearly, this would hinder rather than promote innovation, although it might create new incentives to fund basic science, at least for a while until all nature's laws are discovered. Because the laws of nature are theoretically a limited set, whereas their potential uses are a likely unbounded set, the incentive is properly put at the application end, rather than at the discovery end. Rewarding discovery would front load scientific discovery, encouraging rapid discovery of nature's laws, but then foreclose future rewards as the discoveries slipped into the public domain, and all future technologies based on any natural law discovered would only become worth pursuing once the patents expired.

Problem Areas in Intellectual Property Theory and Practice

I have argued extensively that the treatment of software in intellectual property law reveals a problematic distinction between the realms of patentable and copyrightable subject matter. The dichotomy between the subject of patent and that of copyright hinges upon a tenuous distinction between those things deemed primarily utilitarian, and those deemed "expressive" or primarily aesthetic. The split seems to be between the pleasurable and the useful. I have argued that this distinction is a false dichotomy. All novels, works of art, machines, and processes are expressions: intentionally-created, man-made objects. The real difference has only been that the various media for these expressions have historically been quite different. Machines "do things" as do processes, whereas expressions, whose uses are primarily aesthetic, are passive – or they were until computers came along. Computers meld the aesthetic with the useful. They are books that do things, or machines that express beauty. It's not that computers are an entirely new sort of thing, but rather that the original distinction between these two types of expression is suspect.[7]

The idea/expression dichotomy, on the other hand, is perfectly rational. The purpose of intellectual property law is to encourage innovation, discourage secret-keeping, and to move new knowledge into the public domain after a period of time. By recognizing that ideas cannot be "owned," intellectual property laws keep open the realm of scientific inquiry, even while providing legal protections and economic incentives for new technologies.

It is the particular expression of an idea, not the idea itself, which can be monopolized, and then only for a limited period of time. This encourages a never-ending cycle of new inventions, like new and better mousetraps. Protecting bare ideas, on the other hand, would grant a monopoly on the general idea of mousetraps and prevent innovation or invention of *all mousetraps* but one for the term of a patent. Ideas, after all, cannot be proscribed. The law recognizes this. There is simply no containing them. As some have proclaimed, they "want to be free."[8] But we can regulate expressions. The law regulates other sorts of expressions including speech (to a degree), so it can regulate expressions that are texts, or works of art, or machines and manufactures. The idea/expression dichotomy is not merely economically and legally rational, but philosophically supported by simple facts of the world. Ideas are products of the mind, whereas their expressions are products of the world outside our minds.

We could quibble and say that ideas are also intentionally created, man-made objects. This would be a perfectly sensible materially reductionist view of mental processes. I'm not going to argue this plausible assumption, but rather take the pragmatic view and appeal to our experience. There is an experiential distinction between ideas and their expressions that justifies their distinct treatment by the law of intellectual property. Simply put, I can hold an idea in my head and never express it in the world. Others might hold that idea too, but we cannot know if they do until they express that idea in some medium, whether written, spoken, by model, or by machine. Thus, I'll say that ideas are the intentions themselves upon which intentionally-created, man-made objects (expressions) depend. There is no need at this point to worry about the metaphysical reality or substance of ideas because neither the law nor public policy depends upon that. Rather, the common-sense, pragmatic distinction suffices for our purposes.

The institution of intellectual property is, in fact, a highly pragmatic invention, despite its sometime justification on Lockean/moral grounds. I have argued extensively that it is unlike other forms of property in very important ways that impact notions of *justice* when we choose to develop or alter laws like those of patent or copyright. Property rights over things like hammers or houses are *grounded* in the brute facts of possession and occupation. Some call these natural rights. These sorts of rights are not the creations of positive law, but in order to be just, positive law (enactments) must coincide with these natural (or grounded) rights.[9] The old adage that possession is nine-tenths of the law is true. Most property law recognizes that the fact of possession precedes other claims, and the presumption of ownership that flows from possession is difficult to overcome. Enactments provide instruments like deeds and titles, and formalize the pre-legal facts of possession into legal claims of ownership. I have argued, as have others, that enactments that are founded upon recognition of the legitimacy of possession as a basis for ownership claims are enactments that are *grounded* in brute facts of the world pre-legally. Legal systems or laws that are so-grounded are *just* and those that attempt to usurp or undo grounded rights are *unjust*. Thus a legal system that names all property claims to be "theft," for instance, would be unjust and worthy of replacing.

But what of intellectual property claims? Are they grounded like claims over hammers and houses? Clearly they are not. While we could easily make the case that the invention of, labor upon, possession of, or improvement of a piece of property grounds claims to that token, there is no sense in which any of these acts confers any natural or grounded claim over copies of that token. Unlike real estate or moveables, there is simply no way to exclude others from possession of the types, so claims over each copy of a token, without some prior grounded claim such as by manufacture or prior possession of those particular tokens, cannot be pre-legal or pre-ethical. For these claims, we need to have, and have enacted, positive laws. Even under a Lockean perspective of intellectual property law, while one might argue that the intellectual labor involved gives rights of profit for copies of the type, no theoretical justification grants either practical or moral claim to *possession* of all copies of the type. A new, positive legal scheme is necessary to ensure that the author or inventor profits, and that unlicensed copiers are punished. Such a new scheme is necessarily unlike schemes that protect ownership of land and moveables over which rights of possession and thus ownership claims are more clearly *grounded*. Thus, we have seen the recent emergence of intellectual property law, which creates rights not otherwise natural or grounded, and which is based primarily upon economic efficiency and pragmatic concerns rather than on notions of justice.

Do Genes Fit any Current Notion of Intellectual Property?

Each instance of the un-engineered human genome is a naturally-occurring object. Its existence as an abstracted ideal which is instantiated in you, me, and every other human, in its present form has no element of the type of expression described above. There is no mixing of labor with any present human genome's form, nor is there any human intention involved. By contrast, works of authorship and inventions are expressions of ideas. All copyrightable and patentable objects are intentionally-produced man-made objects and they are not merely ideas. Your DNA, or mine, or any other non-engineered being, is not an expression according to this description of intellectual property, and neither is any naturally-occurring subset of a genome (such as a gene or a SNP).

There are things we call "expressions" associated with genes, and this perhaps confuses things a bit. For instance, genes become *expressed* through phenotypes. Every genetically-based feature of our appearance, development, and metabolism is an *expression* of our genetic makeup. This is the scientific terminology, and the term "expressed" as used by scientists is very different from either the legal term of art or our colloquial use of the term. Expressions in the realm of intellectual property law, as we have seen, are products of intentions. The distinction between a drop-cloth used for painting and a Jackson Pollock painting is that the former consists of accidents, none of which was meant to comprise a work of art, whereas the latter is entirely the product of an attempt to create art. The drop-cloth is not an expression, and cannot be copyrighted, whereas the intentional product – a paint-splatter painting – is copyrightable because it is an expression. Nature is replete with intentional products, though most are human artifacts. We need not delve into the intelligence of other creatures to agree that things like bird nests and termite mounds are not self-organizing elements of the natural world so they are expressions of a sort given that they are products of some intelligence altering the world. We might properly call these things expressions, though we would doubtless not extend any intellectual property protection beyond humans for now. The relevant distinction between those things that are "naturally occurring" and those that we call "expressions" is the mixing of intention (or labor) with some alteration of the natural world. This is a distinction which differs from the idea/expression dichotomy, and which underlies all of intellectual property law.

Unaltered products of nature are not expressive, but they can be made into expressions through some intentional alteration. We may also create new expressions *based upon* products of nature or *about* them. Thus, a poem about, or a painting of, a tree is an expression. Even a photograph of a tree is an expression given that the photographer mixes his or her own intention, through choosing the angle, aperture, and by making decisions about exposure, colors, and so on, when developing, printing or otherwise displaying the photo. The tree is not expressive, but can become the subject of an expression. We also mix intentions with naturally occurring objects which then become patentable. In fact, every machine is the alteration of some natural product, like wood, steel, or ore, with some intention. Somewhere along the way, distinctions that were once clear became blurred and led us to gene patents. Patents first issued over new life-forms which are at the boundaries of these mixtures of types of expressions, where living things have been altered, and the line of cases discussed before brought us to patenting genes themselves. It started with plant patents for intentionally created hybrids of existing plants. It continued through patents for genetically engineered organisms, and then a leap was taken to unaltered genes themselves. While there are some generally expressive elements involved in many gene patents, the reasoning behind the extension of patents over isolated genes or gene fragments based upon those expressive elements is flawed.

The genes that are the subjects of gene patents are always expressed in some manner in a patent application. A diagram of a molecule, for instance, is an expression of the molecule just like a picture of a tree is an expression. A representation of a genetic sequence with the letters that represent its base pairs (. . . CATTCCGG . . . , for example) is also an expression of that genetic sequence. But while a photo or a painting of a tree is a unique expression worthy of intellectual property protection, the diagram of a molecule and the string representing the gene sequence cannot be granted protection. This limitation is recognized in intellectual property law and precedent. Chemical formulas, for example, or natural laws, cannot be copyrighted or patented. The seminal Supreme Court case *Diamond v. Diehr*,[10] specifically excluded from patentability "laws of nature, natural phenomenon and abstract ideas." The reasoning is obvious: granting a monopoly over those things precludes their application by others for useful purposes as we discussed above, and there is no justification for rewarding someone with a monopoly for finding something rather than creating it. But this limitation also necessarily excludes protection of certain expressions, where those expressions are the standard means of representing those laws of nature or abstract ideas. There are only a limited number of ways we might express a particular molecule through models or formulas, and granting anyone an exclusive right over the representation of a product of nature would preclude others from utilizing that law of nature or natural product in useful ways. Moreover, the protection would be un-usefully limited.

Suppose we granted a patent or copyright over the depiction of a water molecule, either through text or picture. What would be the extent of the protection? Because the product underlying it is naturally-occurring, the protection could not extend to water itself, but only to that particular representation of the water molecule: some combination of H's and O's with some feature expressing that there are two hydrogen atoms and one oxygen. There may well be hundreds of ways we could depict the molecule, but it would unnecessarily burden the institutions of science to force scientists to use new methods of depicting natural phenomena so as to avoid infringing the protected expressions. Moreover, it would not serve the purposes of intellectual property law to protect these sorts of expressions. It would not promote innovation, it would only threaten to hinder it.

Patents granted on representations of genes and genetic sequences are just like patenting a depiction of the water molecule. Both are representations of naturally-occurring products, and while there is certainly some human intention involved in representing these natural products, it isn't of the sort that warrants intellectual property protection, nor of the sort that encourages innovation. The discovery of something natural and depiction of that thing using a common scientific notation is not a unique expression worthy of intellectual property protection, and gene patents have confounded this long-standing judicial limitation on the reach of the patent law. This does not mean that no innovations in genetic technologies can be protected. Just as there are numerous means of protecting innovations in chemical engineering or automobile manufacturing, where natural products are put to new and useful purposes, so patents are available for applications of newly discovered knowledge about the genome.

What CAN Properly be Patented?

Many gene patents are perfectly valid both legally and ethically. All valid patents use products of nature in some form, but they do not extend to protect the naturally-occurring parts of the invention. Most patents on new chemicals involve not just a patent on the new compound, but also a patent on the process of synthesizing the compound. These sorts of patents provide guidance for how gene patents can legally issue and still also promote innovation. New genes could of course be patented if they are man-made. New combinations of genes can also be patented if they are the products of human intention. Thus, genetically engineered life-forms or genetically modified life-forms arguably can be justly patented. "Knock-out" mice like the Harvard "OncoMouse™" were created through genetic engineering to provide useful models for studying human diseases in animal studies. The OncoMouse™ is a new invention, developed by the mixture of human intention with something from the natural world, creating something new, at least in part. There are certainly non-engineered elements of genetically-engineered creatures, none of which warrant patents, but the new parts, the inventive parts, are proper subjects of patent protection. The use of genes in genetic engineering, and the identification of those genes, is encouraged by the ability to get patents on genetically modified or engineered life-forms. Numerous new and useful life-forms have been created for commercial and laboratory use requiring first the identification of genes and their functions. There is every reason to believe that there will be significant pharmaceutical value in creating these new life-forms and their products. If we outlawed the patenting of naturally-occurring genes tomorrow, there would still be plenty of incentive to use naturally-occurring genes in new inventions that *could* be patented. This would put pressure on the creation of downstream inventions (technologies utilizing scientific discoveries), rather than encouraging upstream "squatting" which occurs now.

Many gene patents issue now in which the current use of the gene is in merely finding the same gene. This is quite absurd. It is like patenting the element iron, and then claiming that the use of iron is in finding iron, or patenting the Rock of Gibraltar and then claiming that the utility of the patent is in locating the Rock of Gibraltar. I could go on, but you get the point. The great potential utility of genes for science and commerce comes from the role that genes play in the development and metabolism of living organisms. Once we fully understand how each gene relates to health or other useful phenotypic features, we can do things like cure diseases, fix infirmities, develop new and useful organisms to produce drugs for us, or understand the ways that drugs interact with different creatures or individual metabolisms. By granting patents over the genes themselves, as in the case of Canavan's disease or other naturally-occurring genes, we are clogging up the system upstream, discouraging the useful work of creating cures, and putting undue obstacles on those who wish to do the hard work of understanding the natural utility of genes in the wild and use that knowledge to create something new. Moreover, it is contrary to the law and spirit of patent.

Patents should be available to those who do the tough work of applying the discoveries of the roles, uses, and functions of genes to new technologies. This is the case with all of chemical engineering. None of the naturally occurring elements on the periodic table may be patented, but every day new chemical inventions and processes are patented. Patents issue not only for the newly created chemical compounds which do not appear in nature, but also for the processes by which they are extracted or synthesized, if they are non-obvious, novel, and useful. The same could be true for genetic technologies. While the raw gene cannot be lawfully patented as a product of nature, new and useful processes for utilizing naturally occurring genes can be patented through developing new and beneficial therapies, pharmaceuticals, and so on.

Analogize the current situation involving gene patents to a hypothetical situation involving the periodic table of elements. In that hypothetical analogy, the periodic table of elements has suddenly been completely "mapped" and every element discovered, identified and placed into its current configuration on the periodic table. The discoverers of each element then immediately start applying for patents on individual elements. The patent for hydrogen, for instance, lists the utility of the patent as including its "use for the finding of hydrogen in the environment" as its primary utility. The patent issues before various other uses of hydrogen in chemical engineering are discovered, including for instance "as a gas useful for lifting dirigibles" or as a means of "hydrogenating various foods," or even "for use, in combination with the element oxygen in producing water." Now, the owner of the patent for hydrogen can sit back and collect royalties on all of these various uses if someone wishes to pursue them despite the costs of licensing, or the patent owner may enjoy a monopoly on the creation of the technologies putting hydrogen to use if he or she wishes to take the time of inventing useful applications. But there is no particular hurry. The monopoly lasts 20 years, and dirigibles and hydrogenation may just have to wait until the discovery lapses back into the public domain. Clearly, this would not be ideal and would hinder innovation, defeating the purposes of intellectual property laws, and running counter to both their letter and their spirit.

Genes and the Law: Where Do They Fit?

As I have argued, the law of intellectual property can be flexible. It is not grounded in any brute facts of the world, but it is *guided* by some brute facts. The idea/expression dichotomy, for instance, guides the development of intellectual property laws. Because nothing grounds intellectual property rights, we may choose to grant them or eliminate them without violating principles of justice, but we may not break the idea/expression dichotomy justly. Economic efficiency, and our concerns with upholding the purposes of the intellectual property laws we choose to create, suggest that granting monopoly rights over products of nature would be inefficient, unwieldy, and unwise, but would it be unjust? In fact, intellectual property law might well be beyond the realm of justice. It may best be debated as an economic tool, helpful for promoting the creative and useful arts, but neither dependant upon considerations of justice, nor affecting them. However, where intellectual property law runs afoul of the brute facts regarding the freedom of ideas, it may tend toward injustice. Gene patents seem inclined in that direction.

In previous works, I have suggested that we could eliminate patent law and create a unified means of intellectual property protection recognizing the error of the dichotomy between works of authorship and other utilitarian creations. I recognize that this is only a very remote possibility and not a likely development in the near future. Too much now depends on patents and their value to our economy and institutions. But if we keep the patent system, the least we can do is ensure that it functions rationally and within the limits the legislature and judiciary have set for it, as well as that it remains consistent with its purposes to encourage innovation. Consistent with those limits and those purposes, patents for genes in their raw form should not issue. Isolating them is not enough, it isn't innovative, and amounts in practice to mere "squatting" rather than innovation of the type promoted by the patent law. Even without arguing about the justice of gene patents, we can see their ill-logic. We must then either fix the system, altering the law of patent so that naturally occurring products (like hydrogen, for instance) could be patented, or recognize that the PTO has overstepped its authority and reign it in legislatively or judicially. But justice could also be implicated when intellectual property regimes tread on other rights that might exist over categories of objects suddenly deemed patentable. If, for instance, ideas were deemed worthy of patent or copyright, and not simply their expressions, this would curtail our autonomy and our privacy, and would arguably tread upon a "commons" – the realm of ideas. We'll consider this possibility later as it suggests not just that patents for genes are illogical and stretch the existing categories of intellectual property beyond reason, but that they may well be unjust.

Although genes are not properly or justly patentable or copyrightable (as neither an aesthetic nor utilitarian expression), they may well fit into other property schemes. Might we argue that *your* unique genes are your property, and *my* genes are mine? Property schemes and laws have existed long before intellectual property regimes have, and as I have argued above and elsewhere they are grounded in brute facts of possession. We will look below at whether and to what extent existing property laws might apply to claims over genes, and also explore things that are not generally considered ownable as part of the so-called "commons." We'll then see whether genes fit into any of these existing classifications, and what that might imply for gene patents, ownability, personal identity, and global concerns over the practice of bio-prospecting of genetic materials in our species and others.

7 | DNA AND THE COMMONS

We have discussed a bit the various modes of existence for property, ranging from intellectual property to moveables and real property (land). As I have argued, and as is apparent through history and legal institutions, occupation and possession of land and moveables create prima facie presumptions of ownership. These customs are rooted in brute facts recognized by social and, eventually, legal norms. The facts of possession and of generally recognized indicia of ownership give rise to valid claims of property rights over these sorts of objects once legal institutions form. On the other hand, the physical ability to exclude others from possession, which is absent from the realm of ideas (except for mere secret-keeping, to an extent), makes intellectual property regimes necessarily creations of positive law, ungrounded in any way in the world of brute facts of possession. Thus, we may generally devise intellectual property laws as we see fit and consistent with our pragmatic goals of encouraging innovation or Lockean notions of intellectual labor and morality, as well as providing access to new innovators in due course.

Currently, non-engineered human DNA is being patented.[1] We have seen that those patents do not fit accurately into any currently accepted scheme of intellectual property protection. Now we should consider 1 whether DNA fits into other forms of property protection (land, moveables, chattels, etc.) 2 whether DNA warrants a new and unique form of property protection, or 3 whether DNA belongs to the class of objects we generally consider to be "the commons."

Once we answer these questions we will better be able to determine whether there are any *bona fide* ethical problems flowing from non-engineered gene patents, and what alternatives may exist. We may decide that, even if no current scheme of legal protection suffices to secure an individual's rights over his or her own genes, some new form of property-like protection ought to exist. Such a property right could protect the rights of individuals or it may even protect "discoverers" of wild-type (non-engineered) genes. Current schemes of patent protection for genes are entirely new, unwarranted by precedent, and utterly aberrant in applying the law of patent. Nonetheless, it bears examining how intellectual property schemes might serve as guidance for new forms of intellectual property protection for genes, if indeed those genes fit into classical dimensions of intellectual property.

Current Schemes of Intellectual Property Protection

Genes are very much like expressions except for one major, legally and philosophically relevant distinction. While the type/token distinction present in other forms of expression argues for classifying genes as similar to other expressions, they are not the products of human intention. As I have argued before, however, deciding that something is an expression does not determine whether it is properly copyrightable or patentable given that both types of objects are expressive. The determining factor is actually: is its usefulness more utilitarian or more aesthetic? Machines are expressive of ideas as are books and the words in books, and there are types and tokens for each. The blueprint of a machine is a representation of the type, while the individual machine is a token. Reproducing a patentable object without license violates the patent-holder's property rights just as reproducing a work of authorship without license violates copyright. We have made pragmatic decisions to grant more latitude for potential overlap of aesthetic expressions than for primarily utilitarian expressions. We have also decided to move primarily utilitarian expressions more quickly into the public domain than primarily aesthetic ones. These decisions reflect pragmatic concerns, dictated by societal priorities rather than by any natural right over types. Perhaps this dichotomy reflects our Protestant roots in preferring utility over mere aesthetic pleasures.

Current schemes of intellectual property protection reward human inventiveness. Copyright rewards aesthetic inventiveness, and patents reward technological inventiveness as opposed to scientific discovery. Scientific discovery has been historically rewarded through the institutions of science, and the rewards include prestige, grant monies, faculty appointments, fame, and recognition. The only time that genes fit this model is when they are modified. Genetic engineering is the process of bringing human inventiveness to bear on the medium of genetic material. Unlike sexual reproduction, genetic engineering has as its primary purpose the creation of new life-forms with new, specifically determined, genetic structures, guided by the current state of scientific knowledge about the roles of specific genes. Genetically modified creatures are thus patentable subject matter as the *Chakrabarty* decision and its progeny correctly establish. What these cases cannot establish, absent a wholesale rewriting of the patent code, is that wild-type human genes, unmodified by human intention, are somehow patentable. Nonetheless, this is exactly what the *Moore* decision, as interpreted by the actions of the Patent and Trademark Office, has established. Namely, we now live in a world where more than 20 percent of human genes are now literally owned by patent holders, held by corporations, research institutes, and universities.[2] This recent change shows that the law shifts to reflect changing priorities. There are other historical examples of this sort of flexibility.

At one time in the US, societal priorities did not compel us to protect names. When those priorities changed so that Congress passed the Lanham (Trademark) Act (title 15, chapter 22 of the United States Code), a new form of protection for already existing expressions began. We may decide that wild-type genes warrant such a step, and that some new form of intellectual property protection ought to be created for genes so that those who discover them, although they do nothing inventive to create them, may nonetheless stake out this territory as their own. If we do this we will radically change one of the primary characteristics of intellectual property law.[3] We will reward discovery of existing products of nature rather than invention of some new expression. Unless we decide for some reason that genes are the sorts of things that one may not properly "own" in any such way, we could surely change the positive law of intellectual property and expand it this way. As mentioned above, there is one significant parallel between genes and other forms of intellectual property, namely the type/token distinction, or what patent attorneys call the idea/expression dichotomy. Except that the type, which is in the case of genes the string of base pairs, is not an idea. It is a natural product of evolutionary processes completely unguided by intention. The 99.6 percent of DNA we share with each other includes the nearly 25,000 genes that comprise our species' make-up, and define us against all other species. We are all benefactors of evolution and not of intelligence nor of design. The only way we could argue that genes are expressions would be to accept some notion of an intelligent designer as the genesis of life. If that were the case, then patents are being granted to the wrong party, and God has a heck of an infringement suit to bring!

So genes cannot be covered by existing schemes of intellectual property law, even though the law currently erroneously applies patent to wild-type genes. They are not expressions and they are not inventions either. This does not rule out the possibility that genes fit into some other novel form or interpretation of other types of property. As we have touched on above, things are owned in a wide variety of ways.

Existing Forms of Property Protection

Property includes anything that may be possessed, as distinct from intellectual property which may not be possessed under any normal interpretation of possession. In other words, property law covers tokens. The possession of a token excludes another's simultaneous possession of that token in exactly the same way. This is true even for real property. While real property may be jointly possessed, each instance of possession occurs in a slightly different way. For example, real property may be possessed by occupation of that land, flat, or building, but no two possessors occupy that property in exactly the same way. So, too, a titled possession of real property, whereby a possessor is granted some document signaling a legal or institutional form of possession, indicates either a sole, joint, or several possession, or even some limited form of possession such as an easement. However, no two possessors may occupy any single portion of the possession to the total exclusion of another possessor, nor may they, by virtue of brute facts, simultaneously occupy the same portion of the possession precisely, even while title recognizes their right to do so.

This is important because it indicates how the social institutions of possession track brute facts. The facts of possession and occupation necessarily dictate the law that recognizes those facts. Each possessor of a joint custodial piece of real property must nonetheless exercise some continued dominion over his or her real property to the exclusion of non-title potential possessors (those who might "squat" on the land), or risk losing legal recognition of his or her possession through institutions of ownership. Setting aside issues of "ownership," because human genes are possessed by each member of the human species, there is no way to exhibit such exclusivity, nor to prevent others from possessing the genes each of us has. Genes differ from real property the same way that intellectual property does. Possessing genes, like possessing ideas, is non-rivalous. Importantly, the very fact that we share roughly 99 percent of our genes enables us to interact socially because it causes us to be members of the same species, with similar capacities, desires, needs, proclivities, and a shared history.

Possession of moveables and chattels works similarly. Ordinarily, possession is the clearest indicator of ownership, and the social institution of legal ownership tracks the brute facts associated with possession. My possession of a certain object ordinarily excludes that of another person and force, or some gifting, exchange, or other socially recognized manner of shifting possession, is necessary to alter the original state of affairs. Again, genes don't work this way. My possession of a certain gene is both non-exclusive and non-rivalous. My possessing it doesn't mean you cannot also possess the identical gene, nor does my possessing it prevent you from enjoying its benefits (or harms). Moreover, my possession is entirely unintentional on my part. Most forms of possession become legally recognized forms of ownership due to human intention. One cannot ordinarily "accidentally" own something. One presumably also cannot also unknowingly own something. Social norms as reflected in the law thus encourage "responsible" ownership by allowing for adverse possession of objects or land by those who exhibit responsible, knowing indicia of ownership despite prior possession by another where that prior possession was irresponsible. In sum, possession and ownership require at some level some knowledge and intent to be maintained against adverse claims. Finally, possession and ownership of real property and moveables, all of which are tokens, necessarily involves either actual exclusion of others from possession, or some right to exclude, which may yet be overcome by some indication of the prior possessor's failure to responsibly demonstrate that possession or vigorously exclude others.

Which brings us to the problem of genes. While we are all composed of cells directed in their development and metabolism by genes, we possess the tokens and the types differently. That is to say, we all share the types in common, at least to the extent that our genes are generally identical in structure. Even single-nucleotide polymorphisms are not unique to any particular individual, although the sum of all single-nucleotide polymorphisms (SNPs) in a given person is statistically likely to be unique. These alterations in single base pairs occur in populations, or in families, or even in random individuals, but nothing excludes them from occurring tomorrow in yet another individual. My possession of a particular gene, or a particular SNP does nothing to exclude another's similar possession. In fact, this possession is typically completely unknown to the possessor, unless he or she has used some sort of technology to scan his or her genome either partially or fully.[4]

Recognizing the type/token dichotomy in genes makes it clear that our possession of a particular gene only extends to the limited boundaries of our body, and not to the type which is shared by others of the species, or even beyond the species, or which at least is not excluded from possession by others. So what if anything might we be said to "own" or at least possess in regard to ourselves? Social norms, laws, rules, and generally recognized ethical principles seem to capture a sense of this in protecting our rights, to some extent at least, over the boundaries of our bodies and their immediate vicinities. Invasions into our bodies and their immediate vicinities defy some right, be it a property right or a privacy right, but once some part of us *leaves* our body, any claim over it ordinarily disappears (assuming that the means of extracting the sample was non-violent, consensual, and not accidental).

All of this seems to indicate that genes do not fall under typical categories of property. Their possession is ordinarily non-exclusive, non-rivalous, and non-excludable even where it may be accidentally exclusive. Much of the confusion in the law regarding the possession and patentability of genes seems to stem from an unwarranted conflation of the types and tokens associated with tissues and genes, thus conferring on those who come to possess a particular token of a gene by virtue of some release or consent the simultaneous ability to control the expression of that gene (the type) in ways that the original possessor never could (as in the *Moore* case). This is clearly anomalous in the law. No other type which is simply discovered can be owned in this way. Under existing intellectual property schemes, in order to come to "own" a type (like a copyright or patent) one must mix one's own intention or intellectual labor with some naturally-occurring item and create something new. Nothing about the ontology of genes warrants extending this new form of ownership over this particular type. It could well be that we will decide that DNA warrants a new form of protection to encourage innovation, but it clearly does not fit into existing forms of intellectual property or other property protection.

Brute Facts and Genes

How do genes, DNA, humans, and persons relate to each other, and to what extent do analogies to other types of property rights hold? We have clarified a few things. For instance, genes are not expressions of the sort that have been afforded intellectual property protection. In their wild state, they are not the products of human intention and thus should not be given intellectual property protection. They are natural products, resulting from evolutionary forces, but connected with our individuality, personhood, and identity like no other thing. There is no analogy between genes and expressions, but other analogies might be appropriate. Genes are a necessary element of individual human identity and our identity as a species, and some subset of our genes is necessary for personhood. Here's what we can say with confidence, though we'll have to work out the implications for rights, duties, and obligations which might flow naturally from these facts.

A small portion of our DNA, maybe 1 to 2 percent (including genes, SNPs, and copy-number variants), makes us uniquely who we are. A SNP, in which a single base pair is altered, is enough to cause diseases or other less harmful identifiable traits. Even identical twins may have these SNPs that result in one differing in vital ways from the other. It is not uncommon in identical twins for one to suffer from Tourettes or some other illness or condition which makes the two differ in marked ways. Most of our genetic code is shared among us, yet these individual minor changes are enough to make us unique. The sum of the combinations of genes shared among us, each instance of which may have minor variations, and all of the unique bits of our individual genomes help to make us who we are phenotypically. These phenotypic variations also change by interacting with the environment, which can alter expression of genes throughout the body.

So how do these genes relate to you? They are not the products of our intention, though they do in many ways make us who we are. Does this tight correlation between genes and identity imply some right over the appropriation of that part of your genome that is *uniquely* yours? You have not mixed your labor with your genes, so why should you have any ownership interest in them? Is being a necessary element of your identity enough to confer some personal right of control over their use? Unlike real property or moveables, there is no necessary disruption of your possession in the appropriation of genetic material or information by another person. There is no trespass in the traditional sense in my finding a flake of your skin, for instance, decoding your genotype, finding something clinically useful, and then making a million dollars from some medical product. You haven't been deprived of any property and I haven't violated your bodily autonomy, so what if anything has been taken from you? Has any right been violated?

The fact that it does not seem like trespass to use one's genome or genes because that use appears not to deprive them of some property could be the reason we are now operating under a system where genes are treated as intellectual property which is also typically considered to be non-exclusive and non-rivalous. However, DNA and genes are clearly not like any other intellectual property and they fail essential qualifications for that category given they are not the products of human intentions. They are also not like real property or moveables in that use or appropriation of genes does not require giving up something tangible, nor does it require a trespass or the deprivation of any possessory interest on the part of the individual whose genes are appropriated. It seems that genes fall outside of the realm of the sorts of ownership interests we typically make or acknowledge. While genes are a part of us, even to the degree that they or subparts of them may be unique to us and necessary for our identity, we do not own them in any of the ways in which we own anything else. This leaves open a couple of possibilities. One is that there is another form of ownership unique to genes. Another possibility is that ownership is the wrong paradigm for genes and that some other social object covers the relations between persons and genes.

The Human Genome in general is a form of commons. It is jointly possessed by every member of the species and this is a matter of brute fact. There is no means by which it can naturally be enclosed, it is non-exclusive and non-rivalous, and my possession of a particular SNP, gene, or combination of these does not deprive others of their possession or use of those SNPs and genes. If we begin granting exclusive use over portions of the genome, then we have certain anomalous and practically ridiculous results. Having babies would actually technically violate a patent if that baby carries a patented gene given it is the result of an unauthorized reproduction. Whether or not it is actually enforced, this would clearly be an untenable scheme. Simply put, we can analogize genes to water, air, and other resources considered to be part of the commons, and these analogies are *pre-ethical*. They are grounded in brute facts of existence. Like water and air we might bottle them up, but we can never do so in a way that naturally excludes their use by others, at least not in their natural or unmodified state.

There seem to be no brute facts which would ground property rights in genes as types, but this does not mean that they can be ethically appropriated for private use. There are rights other than property rights. There are rights to autonomy and privacy, for instance, grounded in the brute facts of bodily integrity. For instance, you don't own your arm, your kidneys, or

even your heart, at least not in ways consistent with other types of ownership. You cannot sell your organs. They are a *part* of you, but they are generally not considered to be alienable property (although certain organs can
be *donated* while the donor is alive). Rights such as autonomy, privacy, and
a right to life arguably emerge from brute facts and relations between
yourself and your body and these rights seem to have nothing to do with
property relations. As a general rule, property relations do not exist between
humans and their parts nor between humans and other humans. Clarifying
the entire ontology of humans, their parts, and relations among them that
preclude property rights is beyond the scope of this work. Suffice it to say
that there are other ways in which rights emerge besides through property
relations, and violations of our autonomy, privacy, or life are deprivations
that we have decided warrant legal protections although they do not involve
property.

Unique Property Protection for DNA?

We have created new forms of property, previously unprotected by the law,
and not grounded in natural or brute-facts methods of control, possession,
or ownership. Intellectual property evolved this way, as purely positive
lawmaking and developed in stages. Trade secrets, then letters patent, copyrights, and lately, plant patents, trademarks and other innovative methods
of protecting inventiveness have been developed. The purpose of these laws
has been to encourage and promote innovation by rewarding innovators.
Because, however, the domain of protection of these new types of property
protection has extended over a realm previously unprotectable, namely the
expression of ideas, a compromise has been made in most of these laws by
limiting the terms of protection. Protections under these new schemes have
varied from strong and short monopolies over expressions, as in the case
of patents, to weaker and longer-term protections for aesthetic expressions.
These various schemes reflect cultural and economic priorities and have
varied greatly over time and among nations. We have felt free to alter the
forms of these protections over time as new economic, cultural, or political
priorities have emerged. We might feel similarly free to devise new modes
of property-like protections to cover genes either in their discovery,
expression, use, or any combination of these. The only mitigating reason
we might choose not to create such a scheme would be if it were to

contradict some other prior existing right over genes. Intellectual property laws covering inventions and aesthetic expressions do not conflict with any other claim of right over ideas. As I have discussed at length, no such claim of right could be grounded in brute facts. New forms of protection granting property or use rights to DNA would be acceptable if no other claim of right by either individuals or groups may be said to be grounded in the brute facts of their existence.

How might such schemes be devised, assuming they don't conflict with any existing claims of right? We can imagine a literally unbounded set of possibilities. We could choose to create something like currently existing intellectual property monopolies for those who discover genes. Like those granted stake-holds in the American west during the great land-rushes, these would be granted on a first-come, first-served basis, to the party responsible for decoding a gene, simply by virtue of publication. The monopoly might be strong, preventing anyone from utilizing that gene in any product, for any length of time we choose. The monopoly could be weak, simply requiring some form of license or other token payment, or even just recognition for the discoverer. It is even possible that we could choose to grant individuals strong rights over that part of their genome that is unique to them. This sort of regime might preserve the property and privacy goals of the laws of personal identity. We can do this, with no consequences for justice, as long as no other right exists over gene types. On the other hand, there may exist other conflicting rights that would therefore implicate concerns of justice and prevent us from simply creating new schemes of ownership without reference to those rights.[5]

If we decided, for instance, that the human genome was a shared resource, we could devise remuneration schemes that benefit all of us, requiring taxes or fees for the use of this shared resource. We could even conceivably decide to treat DNA as copyrightable, if there were no other moral impediments to such a scheme.[6] We might choose to remunerate on the basis of populations, so that where a gene or SNP is uniquely connected with a certain population, then members of that population become jointly rewarded for its profitable use. We might even choose to treat DNA and genes, as long as they are not engineered, as incapable of being owned in any way. We might treat them as a part of the "commons," or that part of the natural world to which every person has access and which cannot be enclosed. Let's explore this option, first looking at the nature of the commons in general, and its theoretical justifications.

The Notion of the Commons

Private ownership of property has emerged as the dominant legal institution covering modes of possession, at least in the western world. Catapulted by the thought of Adam Smith and John Locke, liberal democracies now encourage and support private ownership of moveables, land, and chattels. Legal institutions and social norms which came before them protect individual rights of possession. Ownership implies rights to possess to the exclusion of others, utilize in nearly any way (with the exception of waste, for land), alienate through sale, gift, barter, or disposal, and often to pass on to another at the time of one's death. Over time, the extent of ownable items has grown. Under feudal regimes, land was generally all owned by the sovereign, and individuals possessed land, to varying degrees, at the grant of the sovereign. Even now, in the United States, land owned "in fee absolute" (the fullest sense of land ownership) is still subject to taking by the state under certain conditions. This is called eminent domain and the state is still considered the "sovereign" (but without any notion of divine right).

Limits on possessing real estate, which include the doctrines of waste and adverse possession, recognize natural limits on the possessibility of land. A tenant may essentially only own so much land as he or she may continue to use, improve, and for certain periods of time actually occupy. These limits lead us the notion of the commons. In ancient British law, one could enclose some part of land that was otherwise considered part of the "commons" and thus come to own it. This flows from the notion that an owner is one who utilizes and improves, and owners lose rights of possession if they fail to do either for a sufficient period of time. The commons is an ancient concept in English law, and describes any land that, although it may be owned by one person, is useable by all to some degree. Village greens, pasturelands, rights-of-way, easements, and other similar objects were typical forms of "the commons." Of course, Garrett Hardin famously describes the "tragedy of the commons" as occurring when all feel free to use something held in common, but none considers it his duty to improve or maintain it.[7]

Modern usage of the term is not limited to land, but includes any good or resource, finite in amount or area but often replenishable, and considered to be a "public good" and thus owned in common by all. Examples include lakes, rivers, airwaves, national parks, clean air, the airspace above a certain height, and even sunlight. It seems that there are really two sorts of commons, 1 those that we choose to consider to be public goods, and 2 those that simply cannot be contained and thus are *necessarily* owned by all members of the public in common. The village green is an example of the former, and the radio airwaves are an example of the latter. Let's delve into this a bit before we apply this to the problem of DNA and genes.

The Commons as a Choice

As described above, the English institution of commons involved decisions by landowners, sometimes private, and sometimes the Crown, to set aside certain lands for use by all. These lands, like all lands in England, were owned by someone – either an individual, a family, or the Crown itself. Yet, certain lands were considered to be justifiably made available to "commoners" for use as grazing lands or for other legitimate purposes. The limits on using lands included "waste," which meant that all were under an obligation to use but not ruin the commons. This limit was also applicable to the landowners themselves and all their tenants. Inferring from these limits, and the permissive use of the land by commoners, the overarching concern was to increase utility and to diminish deterioration. The "tragedy of the commons" only results when these twin concerns are not addressed by all users of the land. This model of the commons recognizes also that enclosure may occur, and that private property is a good, but that it must be done consistent with the need for constant improvement and economical use. In the British model, for instance, anyone who could construct a shelter with a roof and a fire in the hearth before sundown could own that shelter, and thus enclose a portion of the commons. This possibility was regulated in 1588 with the Erection of Cottages Act.

The institution of commons by choice encourages efficient use of lands and discourages fallow or unproductive fields or abandoned properties. It allows those who are not part of the regular, propertied economy to develop a means of self-support, and requires some sacrifice by the sovereign and its subjects by relinquishing monopolistic rights over a portion of the land. By choosing to move a portion of otherwise encloseable land into the public domain for the use of those who would otherwise have no means of providing for themselves, the commons by choice embodies the spirit of the social contract. There but for the grace of God, after all, go we all who might become commoners by fate and thus depend upon this institution. In some ways, commons by choice mimics the bargain we make by moving expressions into the public domain, where the monopoly eventually ends and benefits of intellectual property accrue to the public at large. Land that becomes commons by choice similarly reverts to a common ownership, and the commons is a form of public domain from which any and all enterprising and responsible caretakers can nurture further sustenance.

Typically, rights to the commons were also limited to certain activities, such as a right to gather fruits or berries only, to hunt certain animals only, to fish, or just to graze livestock. These sorts of limited rights to the commons are preserved in the US legal system with various rights to graze, harvest wood, or to otherwise utilize national forest lands, for instance. Some things that are in the commons are also there due to choices, but choices made due perhaps to the difficulty of enclosure. Rivers, for instance, could be partitioned, and their "possession" enforced by certain acts or indicia of ownership, but it seems extraordinarily difficult to envision this. The oceans are even more difficult to enclose. Of course, airspace is defended by nation-states but not by individuals. Near space, or that airspace beyond a certain height, is almost impossible to envision defending against trespass, and numerous international treaties recognize this and place it firmly into the commons. But these are still all clearly choices. We can envision complex methods of delineating and enclosing even the oceans, and enforcing possessory rights over them. Elinor Ostrom describes in detail methods and justifications, from a game-theory perspective, of regulating traditional commons in her book *Governing the Commons.*[8]

There are others sorts of things now treated and considered part of the commons which we might say are there due to necessity. They just so happen to be the sorts of thing that one simply *cannot possess.*

The Commons by Necessity

More recently, a class of objects has been considered part of the commons because of the seeming impossibility of enclosing them. Unlike airspace, the airwaves cannot be contained or defended against another's trespass. One who wishes to broadcast on a certain spectrum may do so and only risk the possibility that another person with a stronger transmitter will drown them out. Radio spectra are simply unencloseable. Without regulation, some sort of eventual market might emerge for cooperative sharing of such a commons, but in the interim, the potential for chaos and a chaotic marketplace encourages the emergence of some sort of regulatory framework. Other unencloseable commons might be outer space, and ideas. Once ideas are known, there is simply no way to contain them, and they may not be defended in any way from independent discovery. Even the law of intellectual property recognizes this limitation with the idea/expression dichotomy. Ideas may not be protected under any intellectual property framework, although their expressions clearly are.

Intellectual property law makes a compromise, as discussed above, releasing expressions once contained back into the commons as eventual "public domain." Once a previously protected expression enters the public domain, it too may no longer be contained, not as a matter of necessity (as the expression was once regulated in the intellectual property framework) but rather by choice. Ideas themselves, however, remain in the public domain once released through some expression. The only method of containing ideas is secret-keeping, but this is imperfect and does nothing to prevent independent discovery of those ideas by others, nor is there any legal regime which either punishes or remunerates for independent discovery or use of secrets.

There are certainly *regulatory* frameworks that cover the use of unencloseable commons, but we should not confuse this regulation with enclosure. Outer space is regulated by international treaties, the expression of ideas is regulated by intellectual property law as well as international treaties and organizations like the World Intellectual Property Organization (WIPO), and international waters are similarly regulated. Just because something cannot be enclosed doesn't mean that it should be left totally unregulated. Pragmatic decisions about the use of these commons are made for both moral and economic reasons. The air itself, as opposed to airspace, is regulated by local laws and treaties as well. The Kyoto accords, and numerous other limitations on emissions protect a resource that is both unencloseable and finite. Without regulation, the use of this commons has resulted in diminution of the resource with potentially disastrous consequences. Is it possible that DNA and genes fall under this category of commons?

DNA as a Commons

Commons by necessity exist by virtue of brute facts rather than institutional reality, with the exception of the commons originally recognized by English law. The commons of ancient English law are all private property with caveats. Such commons exist by choice, where something exists over which indicia of ownership may be maintained, but society and individuals make choices to allow use of that property by others. Commons that exist by logical necessity, as described above, are simply uncloseable, although we may choose to define limits to their use and regulate to preserve them. We can pretty easily discern which type of a commons an object falls into by asking whether it is the sort of thing that can be enclosed in any meaningful way. Is DNA or are genes these sorts of things?

Because it is the nature of DNA and genes to propagate, containment seems impossible. Like air (as opposed to airspace) and radio frequencies, or even international waters, it is nearly impossible to conceive how one could exert exclusive control of genes, especially given 1 their presence in reproducing individuals, 2 the fact that they exist across species, and 3 that they evolve without any input by human intention. DNA and genes seem readily to fit into the category of commons by necessity. This, of course, does not mean that they could not be regulated, but it serves as a useful guidepost for determining the legal, practical, and moral issues associated with the use of genes, and any subsequent regulation we might wish to agree to over their use[9].

What potential moral issues relate to the existence and regulation of necessary commons? Considering that they are the sorts of thing which cannot practically be enclosed, and possession and use of which is ordinarily common to all to the exclusion of none, attempts to enclose the commons could be considered a deprivation of some sort of general property, liberty, or other interest held by each member of a community or, in this case, species. Imagine a tax on air, or a levy on sunlight, or some corporation claiming ownership of the open seas and demanding royalties for their use. Imagine a world where ideas could be owned, and thinking ideas held by others was prohibited or subject to fees, taxes, or royalties. These scenarios are dystopian nightmares and not what we would ordinarily consider to even be remote possibilities. Because, however, any necessary commons may be spoiled or wasted by their use, we can imagine and have accepted regulations governing pollution, or building heights, fishing, or the expression of certain ideas for limited periods of time. In fact, there is a moral imperative for some of these regulations given our common rights to enjoy the commons.

The moral dimension of DNA ownership, assuming that it falls into the category of commons by logical necessity, is vast. As a necessary commons, each of us is entitled to its use, no practical means of enclosing it exists, and enclosing it may deprive any or all of us of rights to that commons. The current regime of gene patenting violates both reason and morality. Importantly, it is impossible to enforce a gene patent in any evenhanded way. Technically, each of us carrying a gene that has been patented runs the risk of making unauthorized reproductions simply by virtue of reproducing. When we pass that gene on to our progeny we have technically violated the patent. We might similarly violate a gene patent if we were simply to order a genetic test revealing the patented gene to be present in our own genes. Will we need to pay license fees to the patent holders of our own genes when we get genetic tests? It simply seems unmanageable, and puts each of us in the untenable position of violating patents on things that are already inherent parts of us. The moral quandary of turning every human being into an unwitting patent violator is obvious.

And so what of regulation? I have given examples above of manners in which necessary commons may yet be regulated. In one set of these examples, would-be owners are restrained from certain uses of the commons, and in the other set of examples, a limited set of uses for limited time periods have been allowed over *expressions* of a commons (namely – ideas). Let's consider briefly each of these possibilities, and later we will look in depth at practical considerations involved in encouraging innovation in genetic and genomic research, and how these practical considerations might be taken into account rationally.

Is DNA More like Ideas or Radio Spectra?

If DNA and genes are like ideas, then we might permit some sort of limited ownership over their *expression by others*. This is how the law of intellectual property ordinarily operates. In both patent and copyright, originators of an idea are permitted a limited monopoly over the expression of that idea by another. Is DNA at all like this? Simply, no. The purposes of intellectual property law are to encourage innovation by promoting the development of new ideas, and to move those ideas eventually into the public domain by giving the originator some limited reward. There is no sense in which genes fit this schema. Un-engineered, they are simply not the result of anyone's original thought. They are nobody's ideas. It is not merely that genes are old ideas. They are not ideas at all. They are parts of nature. To illustrate this important point: South Dakota is an idea composed of a layer of social reality superimposed on the brute facts of a piece of land. Devil's Tower,[10] however, is not an idea. It simply is. It juts from the earth in a recognizable shape with or without human intervention. We might have ideas about it, but Devil's Tower preexists any ideas and will likely survive long after the death of our species.

DNA is more like radio spectra, or outer space. These are things that are products of nature, preexisting any human invention, but which we none-theless may navigate, utilize, and over which we may regulate use and enjoyment. Unlike the realm of ideas, DNA is inseparable from its expres-sion. All wild-type DNA necessarily is "expressed" in the biological sense of the term. It always exists in some creature. This is unlike the cotton gin, which did not exist until someone expressed its idea, but only after the idea was dreamed up. And so the manner by which we might regulate genes and DNA should take into account the nature of them both in their wild-forms, as necessary commons, whose enclosure is impossible in any practical way, and which is fundamentally different from the realm of ideas and the domain of intellectual property law.[11]

We can choose to create licensing schemes for uses of those things that are commons by necessity. In fact, we often have to do so once people begin to utilize them. If we do not regulate these sorts of commons, then the tragedy of the commons can occur. Radio spectra become useless, space becomes un-navigable and deadly. When confronted with these sorts of unencloseable yet valuable spaces, we must negotiate ways to use them without destroying them or making them unprofitable. Treaties and laws regulate the usage of space, and we should consider ways to make the human genome available to all for exploration, and to innovate, but without creating the sort of chilled environment the current practice of gene patents is already creating. We can certainly envision regulatory schemes for genes similar to those that exist for other commons by necessity, involving usage rights with fees benefiting the public rather than patent-holders. For the privilege of doing business on a certain band of the radio spectrum, radio station owners pay licensing fees to national regulatory agencies. Nations enter treaties with other nations to further regulate the international conflicts that can arise over the use of radio spectra along common borders. The public ultimately benefits, and those wishing to use the radio spectra benefit by enjoying a more orderly and predictable marketplace. The public also benefits through the collection of licensing fees. A similar scheme might be devised for the privilege of using certain portions of the genome to develop profitable technologies.

Finally we are beginning to get to the root of the philosophical and ethical problem of gene ownership. I have argued all along that before we can sort out any of the related ethical issues, we must first develop a clear ontology of DNA and genes. We must understand what they are and how they relate to individuals, humans, and persons. Only then can we begin to solve the problems of whether they are the sorts of things that can be owned. Some will object to my method, preferring instead to abide by the language and methods commonly employed in ethical reasoning. I contend that ontology and ethics cannot be separated, and are in fact deeply inter-related. No ethical discussion can occur absent some sound work in ontology.

Even for those who disagree with the methodology and philosophical assumptions I have used and based my arguments upon so far, there are a number of compelling, pragmatic reasons why patenting unmodified genes ought to be reconsidered. These pragmatic concerns encompass economics, the institutions and practices of science and scientists, and generally-accepted concerns over individual privacy and autonomy. Let's look at these practical concerns next.

8 | PRAGMATIC CONSIDERATIONS OF GENE OWNERSHIP

Gene patenting is impacting the realm of scientific inquiry, as well as individual rights such as privacy and autonomy. Moreover, there are economic consequences due to the burdens of the patent system on small or emerging biotech companies. We should consider not only the practical effects of the status quo, but also look at what would happen if we decide to alter or abolish the current practice of patenting genes. The marketplace and commerce are impacted, as are more abstract things such as rights, privacy, autonomy, and other more strictly philosophical matters. Let's look at some of the practical consequences of the current situation in both science and industry, and forecast how altering the law might affect each.

Public policy may turn on philosophical issues, but it more commonly turns on the marketplace and commerce. The law of intellectual property was developed as an engine of economic growth, and balances the need for increased public knowledge with private economic incentives. If we alter the practice of granting gene patents we will be affecting the patent portfolios of numerous large companies, universities, and individuals who profit from the current system. Any change requires significant justification as well as some sort of plan to absorb the economic effects. It could well be that some middle path exists so that the impact of losing patents, if we decide that they are unjustly held, is lessened. It could also be that the cost is not worth adjusting the law, and that the injustice of granting property rights over unpatentable objects is worth putting up with for now.

Finally, economic consequences aside, some things are so unjust that our sense of justice demands change regardless of consequences. The institution of slavery was abolished because of its injustice and property "rights" were altered abruptly and without regard to the economic consequences. We should consider at least three possibilities: 1 justice demands eradicating patenting genes no matter what the consequences, 2 justice and economic efficiency demand altering the current system to meet both concerns, or 3 the economic effects of altering or eradicating the present system outweigh both the concerns of justice or economic efficiency, and so the status quo should be maintained. We will explore each of these possibilities with an eye toward actually proposing rational public policy scenarios that could be adopted.

The Evolution of the Institutions of Science

Modern science, until recently, was conducted with little concern for profit. The institution of science as it originated in the modern era through the great Enlightenment scientific societies like the Royal Society, was driven not by the potential economic rewards of scientific discovery but by more esoteric rewards.[1] These rewards included: recognition by peers, university lectureships or other appointments, and partaking in the general onward march of knowledge and innovation. Profits were for technologists, who began to abound in the nineteenth century. People like Thomas Edison could concern themselves with patents and profits, but Sir Isaac Newton, Marie Curie, and James Watson profited us with their discoveries as much or more than they did themselves, at least monetarily speaking. Science moves forward by more or less idealistic forces and has done so since its inception. Its combination with industry is a rather recent turn of events and hinges upon a few notable changes in the way that universities treat science in the US. Let's briefly look at the history of science in the US following World War II to the present day and ask how profits became mixed up with academic research to begin with. We'll also consider whether other successful models for moving from discovery to invention exist.

Before World War II, science was conducted at universities, funded generally by tuition and university endowments that paid for labs and materials for their researchers. There was no such thing as "big science" yet, not of the type that was necessitated by the war. The threat to civilization posed by Nazi science, which was organized nationally and well-funded, and which developed productive new technologies geared toward war as well as a research program to develop an atom bomb, required a US response. We all know what resulted: the greatest big-science investment ever made brought hundreds of scientists and thousands of supporting staff to government-sponsored laboratories working under deep secrecy. The

Manhattan Project lasted years and succeeded at its goal, proving that scientists working with government support could achieve monumental things. Following the war, Vannavar Bush, who was central to coordinating the Manhattan project, lobbied to create permanent sources of government funding for science. The National Science Foundation and the National Institutes of Health are some of the direct results of Vannavar Bush's efforts to get government involved in funding science through grants and other means of funding for US universities. Although rather removed from the idealized vision laid out in Bush's opus, *Science – The Endless Frontier*,[2] the system that was established was responsible for a number of significant scientific advances in the US post-World War II, and probably is responsible for US scientific dominance, as measured by publications, Nobel prizes, and foreign demand for US scientists, for nearly 50 years.[3]

So how has US science historically benefited technology, and was there a profit motive for pure research? Technology certainly profited by the rapid advance of science in the US, and inventions and patents have flourished since World War II. Until recently, these patents rarely issued to the benefit of the scientists, however. Pure research and technology are two distinct enterprises. In an environment promoted by abundant public money, pure research need not concern itself with the potential profitability of scientific discovery. In fact, the nature of science itself, which concentrates on discovering the fundamental laws of nature, is necessarily not primarily an applied field, at least not typically in any profitable way. Unburdened by worrying about the potential profitability of researching an aspect of nature, scientists are free to pursue any and all inquiry. If they were concerned with profits, they would have to concentrate only on those aspects of nature that might be likely to result in marketable technologies. Whole fields of research are not profitable. Astronomy is not profitable, and neither is most theoretical physics. Billions have been spent on particle accelerators without regard to profit (other than knowledge) from the investment. This sort of science has revealed deep truths about nature, most of which have not profited anyone financially even while there have sometimes been profitable spin-off technologies. These scientific pursuits would never have been conducted privately because of this fact. No investor with any sense would have spent money on looking for quasars or probing the internal structure of the atom. It would have been money down the drain.

Mapping the human genome was another big-science project that used public money to expand the fount of general knowledge without any expectation of monetary return on the investment. The return was supposed to come in the form of advances in health sciences and possibly spin-off biotechnology applications. But by the time the Human Genone Project (HGP) began, things had begun to change in the way science was being pursued, and the US government had begun to grow wary of huge, unremunerated public investment in science. By the late 1980s, large domestic deficits convinced many that expenditures on everything (except defense) needed to be reigned in, and the big truths about the universe seemed less pressing than losing America's prominence in things like auto sales. One of the early US sacrifices of big science was the Superconducting Supercollider, which would have enabled physicists to probe the energies present at the Big Bang and likely allowed them to complete the standard model of particle physics.[4] The US ceded this field of inquiry to the Europeans, who have now finished construction of the Large Hadron Supercollider at CERN which is expected to do what the Superconducting Supercollider would have done.

Because most big-science research was supported by federal funds, until the 1980s there were no available intellectual property rights for scientists involved in such research. The money was publicly provided, and scientific discoveries (unless classified for security reasons) became part of the public domain. Journals and conferences were the media for reporting the discoveries made possible with public money. Intellectual property rights inhered in the government or government agencies sponsoring the research, if at all. Many discoveries never warranted any intellectual property protection because they were just that – discoveries. Inventions were often spin-offs of the pure scientific research, and were pursued independently through publicly-disclosed scientific knowledge made available through public channels to private technologists. In 1980, however, the relations among institutions that had moved science forward in the US, outpacing all other national or private scientific progress for 30 years, was altered significantly. 1980 was the year that Senators Birch Bayh and Bob Dole sponsored legislation that changed the way that public science and the patent system interacted.

The Bayh–Dole Act[5] gave US universities, small businesses, and not-for-profits the ability to hold intellectual property rights on inventions developed with federal funds. This forever changed the ways that research in universities was conducted, and is in no small part ultimately responsible for the current practice of patenting genes. Under Bayh–Dole, new incentives were created for university scientists to engage not just in pure research, but to work with industry (and sometimes even start their own parallel for-profit businesses) to use their science to build individual and university-held patent portfolios that could make pure research directly profitable for all the parties involved. Of course, this has directly affected how various scientific pursuits are perceived given that it has essentially created a profit-motive that was not previously present in university-based research. It has created pressure on universities, which are still the major bastions of pure research, to think of how their resources ought best to be allocated with an eye on developing relations and investments from private industry. In the process, some universities have seen their endowments grow, swelled both by corporate donations and by royalties from patents. Some faculty members have similarly profited, either through corporate partnerships, royalties from their own patents, or spin-off businesses which they have founded or with which they have become affiliated, either as shareholders or serving on boards of directors – often with some unfortunate ethical consequences.[6]

The biotech revolution has been partly fueled by the mad rush for patents and the inherent profitability of medical technologies. Biotech research is a natural nexus for university efforts at "technology transfer" (the buzzword for moving basic research to patentable technologies) and some recent spin-offs from university and federally funded science have become jackpots for universities and researchers.

The Big Business of Biotech, and the Cornucopia of the HGP

As discussed above, the HGP was initially begun as a publicly-funded, old-style big-science project involving dozens of research centers in numerous countries. Universities and their governments from around the world agreed to divide up the work, each sequencing manageable chunks of the three billion base pairs that compose humanity. At the time, sequencing was a slow-moving project, consuming significant time, energy and resources to decipher relatively small sections of the genome. The painstaking work could not have been completed with the technology then available, specifically the sequencing machines and computing power that was then largely lacking, without widespread cooperation by hundreds of labs around the world. Like many big-science projects, however, the HGP resulted in significant advances in related technologies and spawned the *private* equivalent of the HGP, which was originally a competitor but which became a collaborator of sorts, on the part of J. Craig Venter and his company Celera, Inc. discussed in greater length previously.[7]

Unlike most big-science projects, the HGP held the promise of a potentially profitable market for the products of its research, and it therefore encouraged private investment previously unanticipated by those who originally lobbied for starting the HGP. It was assumed that, like the space race, many of the profits that might be reaped from the public investment would come from spin-off technologies such as devices and procedures that would enable more rapid sequencing, as well as downstream patents from patentable inventions enabled by the scientific discovery. As with other similar projects, most of the reward would come through a generally increased wealth of public knowledge, much of which would be useful in preventing, treating, or curing disease. In fact, Celera did develop and patent new and better sequencing technologies, but that was not enough for them. Venter's dream was to give the HGP a run for its money and complete a privately-financed map of the human genome, patenting genes as they discovered them in order to justify the private investment, and to increase the stock value for Celera's shareholders. To some, this model was a triumph for the argument that private investment rather than public tax dollars could achieve better results faster than any governmentally-sponsored bureaucratic boondoggle could. Certainly, Celera's involvement did speed things up considerably given that, by all accounts, after its involvement the speed of sequencing revved up, new technologies emerged and were licensed to others to rapidly sequence genes, and the public version of the HGP, with its eyes on the rear-view mirror watching Celera catching up, ramped up its efforts to achieve its goals more efficiently and quickly. But unlike the relationships between the Apollo program and private industry contractors, the subject of the HGP was ripe for private claims, fueled in part by the Bayh–Dole Act which had opened up patents even for federally-funded science. Whereas Bell Labs never tried to stake claims on parcels of land on the moon, private industry partners as well as universities and researchers began to lay claim to those parts of the human genome that didn't make it into the public domain.

The conflict should have been apparent. The potential market for products that might be created from mapping the human genome was significantly larger than that for potential products from particle physics, astronomy, or the moon program ever could be. The potential consumers of the products of a greater understanding of the human genome, and of locating specific genes, include all of us. Human health was already a multi-billion dollar industry when the HGP was launched, and has been one of the largest beneficiaries of Bayh–Dole, resulting in huge biotech patent portfolios in both universities and private corporations. A publicly-financed HGP would be a potential gold mine of applications for biotech, even without patents for genes. New pharmaceuticals, inspired or directly benefiting from knowledge about the human genome, were virtually assured to come out of the project. The burgeoning field of pharmacogenomics (the study of how different genetic backgrounds effect drug metabolism) was made possible by completion of the HGP and promises, some predict, a bright new age of personalized medicine, producing cheaper, more effective treatments based upon an individual's genes. But the potential of promising spin-off technologies and industries were not enough. One of the troubling caveats of the HGP, at least for private industry, was that all of the knowledge garnered directly through its public version was to become immediately part of the public domain. Celera and others who wished to reap greater profits by claiming not just the rights to technologies derived from discovering new genes, but to the genes themselves, would have to find those genes on their own, and do so before the HGP did. A new frontier was open and a massive gold rush was launched in order to rapidly stake valuable claims before the government found the treasure first, and give it back to the people by putting it into the public domain.

The Marketplace of Genes

Could the genie be put back in the bottle? What does the current marketplace of genes mean, and what difference would it make if we were to abolish the practice of allowing patents on gene sequences? In a study in the journal *Science*, as of 2005 nearly 4,000 genes had been patented, and nearly 2,000 of those were held by Incyte, Inc., a private biotech company.[8] As discussed at length above, most of these patents include claims over the sequence of a gene or gene segment itself, with utility claims often being little more than using the gene sequence as a means of finding the gene. While many of these patents may have been reduced to practice as useful tests for finding or isolating genes, the patents on those sorts of inventions will not be invalidated if we recognized that the claim only encompasses the test, and not the gene sequence itself, nor the sequence's actual *use* in other inventions. If tomorrow we decided that genes themselves could not be patented, there is still a wealth of spin-off technology and patentable uses to which genes could be applied. Patent claims are severable, so invalidating a whole category of claims would leave valid all other valid claims in any particular patent. There would be no wholesale deprivation of property rights, and it would likely spur private investment and public investment in genomic technologies that may otherwise be chilled now due to overbroad patent claims.

By opening back up large swaths of the genome that have had patent claims staked, more innovation could likely be encouraged. The first parts of the genome that were patented were areas around which known genetic diseases lurked, or areas which were suspected to be associated with diseases like Alzheimer's which are likely to have genetic causes. One consequence has been that those wishing to research those diseases may be discouraged from doing so given the potential for litigation or due to the costs of royalties. Unless the parties holding those patents have created something useful out of them, then there is just cause to open back up those parts of the genome so that researchers can develop new technologies. Even if useful inventions have come from those patents, revoking patents on the gene sequences themselves ought not to preclude inventing any useful technologies (again, assuming the use is more than just the "for use in finding" use). Rather, it will encourage developing new and useful parallel technologies relating to those gene sequences rather than preventing competitors from doing the basic research that might lead to useful inventions.

Now let's consider the problem in light of a hypothetical marketplace unfettered by governmental regulations, and examine what might occur if there were no patents for genes. Arguably, patents are a governmentally-sponsored monopoly that would not exist in an unregulated marketplace. So how might competitors in a world without patents secure their profits over medical technologies relating to the human genome? Consider Ronald Coase's theories about economic efficiency. He argued that in the absence of transaction costs, all government allocations of property rights are equally efficient because interested parties will make bargains to correct for externalities. Discussing the allocation of radio spectra, he argued that as long as property rights in those frequencies were well defined, then it really did not matter if at first two stations' signals interfered with each other. The station best able to reap a greater economic gain would have an incentive to pay the other station to not interfere.[9] Can we make the same argument about discoveries and inventions pertaining to them from the human genome? Might an unregulated marketplace allocate resources more efficiently among market players, rewarding those who are best positioned to take products to market without inhibiting discovery by others by eliminating a government-sponsored monopoly?

We can view patents one of two ways: either as a private right, based upon some sort of Lockean view of labor which has only recently come to be protected by positive law, or as a product only of the positive law. Even under the Lockean view, although there is a mixing of labor with the creation of any one token, or any number of tokens, extending that basis of ownership to the *type* or to every possible instance of a token of that type is a stretch. As argued above, in the absence of any positive law, and without legal institutions that can enforce that law, types are only ideas that can be copied at will, and the labor then mixed with the new token is that of the copier, not the inventor. The marketplace for genes as it currently exists, utilizing the government-sponsored monopoly of patents, rewards not inventors but discoverers. The discoverers often do nothing beyond "isolating" the gene they discover, and the mixture of labor that might afford some property right over tokens is utterly absent. Even if the Lockean view of intellectual property rights were logically applied to reproductions of tokens with no mixing of labor on the part of the inventor, it can provide no support for the notion that *discoverers* of genes that already exist attain some sort of property right over all other instances of those genes elsewhere in the world.[10]

The stronger argument for intellectual property law comes both historically and logically from the fact that it is a relatively recent invention, and that it has largely worked as a flexible, new, pragmatic and positive institution meant to encourage innovation and improve economic efficiency. It was created because there was simply no other way to protect the expression of ideas, or to exclude others from expressing them in the absence of a positive legal institution and enforcement mechanisms. So far, it has been pretty successful. There is good evidence that since the development of intellectual property law the world has experienced a rapidly accelerating curve of progress. Most of the technological innovation that has fueled that progress emerged from the western world and was bolstered by intellectual property regimes. But this doesn't mean that all innovation *must* come from intellectual property, nor does it rule out the possibility that some intellectual property schemes may actually impede innovations (e.g, such as when terms of protection grow too long). In fact, large portions of the marketplace are unprotected by intellectual property and some highly profitable products may emerge and flourish with no support at all from intellectual property law. Imagine then a totally free market in which genomic technology proceeds without gene patents. How might such a market function and might it even flourish?

Open Source and Free Markets

Patents are not free market devices. They are government-sponsored monopolies. They are created to control the free marketplace of ideas, and hand to inventors a unique, legal monopoly over every expressive token of their idea. But free markets do exist and have thrived at the cusp of scientific advance and technological development for hundreds of years. Not every scientific advance nor every technological innovation needs patent protection to make profits. Some who have been concerned over the growth of copyright terms have latched onto the growing Open Source movement as a means of combating the sometimes stifling monopolies associated with works of authorship which now enjoy protection lasting much more than a century. The current copyright term, following the Sonny Bono-sponsored copyright extension act, now lasts the lifetime of an author plus an extra 75 years. This extension was granted just as the cartoon character Mickey Mouse™ and his earliest films were about to lapse into the public domain. In the realm of computer technologies, strong and extended copyright protection has made software and other necessary parts of vital machines prohibitively expensive, and so users became trapped by the brand of the machine they purchased into using whatever operating system and its associated software happened to be bundled with it. Users unhappy with what they sometimes perceived as inferior products at outrageous prices started a new marketplace, one in which government-sponsored mono-polies don't stifle innovation, nor do they allow price gouging.

The Open Source movement in software emerged almost immediately, with the first "publicly" distributed programs coming from rising young computer geeks at schools like the Massachusetts Institute of Technology (MIT) and Stanford who traded their software creations for free, improved upon them, and did not consider marketing them for money. Actually, this was "freeware," a precursor to Open Source, and the logical offshoot of other forms of scientific inquiry or tinkering of the sort that science nurtures. Those same geeks went on to write their doctorates, impact the direction of computer science as an academic discipline, and earn fame and notoriety and support for their further research. This was the traditional path of science and some deemed it crude or uncouth to try to earn profits from their science. Richard Stallman, who was a member of the MIT Artificial Intelligence Lab, was one such noteworthy programmer. When companies began emerging to market software, and copyrights issued to protect their profits, Stallman founded the Free Software Foundation and wrote the "GNU Manifesto" which outlined his reasons for developing a free operating system called "GNU" which was free and designed to be compatible with the proprietary Unix operating system.[11]

To support his project of creating robust, free software alternatives to expensive copyright-protected commercial products, in 1985 Stallman created what he called a GNU General Public License (GPL) otherwise known as "copyleft." Stallman published all his new software under the "copyleft" license and it caught on with others. One of the features of the license was that everyone was free to implement it and to refine it as they saw fit. It is a truly free market device and it does not preclude profit-making mechanisms. Instead, it makes these mechanisms the products of freely-entered bargains among parties rather than government-sponsored, one-sided monopolies.

In 1990, Linus Torvalds modified an operating system that had been partially created by Andy Tenenbaum, which Tenenbaum called "Minix." Torvalds completed the operating system, making it a full-fledged competitor to the copyrighted Unix operating system and named it Linux. He released Linux under Stallman's GPL and it is now in widespread use by individuals and corporations as a robust yet lightweight operating system. One of the features of the GPL is that it encourages innovation by users. As a result, products released under it are subject to constant improvement, vetted by a sort of peer review process among other users and developers, and without threat of litigation for violating the original product's copyright for producing unauthorized derivative works. This model has proven to be competitive with typical copyright in the marketplace, and the Open Source movement is growing. In 1997, Bruce Perens penned a manifesto and coined the term "Open Source" and Eric S. Raymond popularized the movement in an essay entitled "The Cathedral and the Bazaar." Commenting on the new movement toward Open Source in software and reflecting on his software engineering career, Richard Stallman noted:

> I could have made money this way, [copyrighting software] and perhaps
> amused myself writing code. But I knew that at the end of my career, I would
> look back on years of building walls to divide people, and feel I had spent
> my life making the world a worse place.[12]

Stallman's approach treated software more like the typical scientific endeavor, improved through openness, testing, and improvement by a community of peers rather than as a business protected by creating legal
barriers to the same motivations.

In 1998 the Open Source Initiative (OSI) was launched as a not-
for-profit company in reaction to the announcement by Netscape that it
was releasing its code for the Mosaic browser to the public. Mosaic had
been the first widely used graphical browser but it was being put out of
business by Microsoft's Internet Explorer. Releasing the source code into
the public domain and being relaunched as a major Open Source initiative
gave Mosaic new life, and it gave the founders of OSI their first opportunity
to take the idea mainstream and prove it as a concept. Within hours of
releasing the source code, fixes and enhancements to Mosaic began to be
posted. Mozilla's Firefox is the result and is a major competitor for Microsoft and Apple's browsers with nearly one-quarter of the market.

Numerous examples of successful Open Source products exist, including
Linux, Apache, Darwin (which is the basis for Apple OS X), Sendmail,
Mozilla/Firefox, OpenSSL, and Perl. These products are successful, captur-
ing significant market share, and proving the basis for profits through
licensing deals and advertising revenue. They prove that Open Source can
make money even without strong intellectual property rights in a marketplace where innovators and customers interact through private contract
rather than by leveraging government-supported monopolies. In many
ways, they mimic the several hundred years of success in the institutions
of science itself which could be argued to be the first major Open Source
initiative. In fact, in science, Open Source enterprises currently abound,
including in biological and genomic initiatives.

Open Source in Biology

As argued above, Open Source essentially amounts to the ideal methods of
the sciences applied to products in the marketplace. It is also analogous to

the means by which once-patented products that already have lapsed into the public domain continue to be marketed, improved upon, and profitable despite the lack of intellectual property protection. There are also many examples of Open Source-style biological science research programs that have proven successful, and that have allowed for and even encouraged downstream profits through new technologies. The HGP itself was conceived as a public domain program, but with the potential for "downstream" patents for new innovations that might have spun-off from the public science. As with other publicly-financed big-science programs, technology was expected to benefit, and profits were likely to benefit private sector partners who would innovate either in the process of discovering the map of the genome, or using information garnered from the project to create new drugs or other technologies. Other genomic and biological science programs have been explicitly created as Open Source projects aimed at keeping the knowledge developed in the public domain and avoiding patentability of new discoveries.

The SNP Consortium and the HapMap Project are two large-scale, international projects whose discoveries may not be patented. The SNP Consortium was established to prevent private industry from cornering the discovery of single-nucleic polymorphisms (SNPs), which are very useful in genetic disease discovery. The more SNPs become patented, the more costly it would be for scientists to work with them in the lab, and the more difficult it would be to research their role in genetic diversity, diseases, and pharmaceutical development. Concerned over these potential barriers, it was actually a group of pharmaceutical companies that agreed to enter into the consortium and create a SNP map that would be in the public domain just as the results of the HGP were to be. In April 1999, companies such as APBiotech, the Bayer Group, AG, Bristol-Meyers Squibb, Co., as well a seven other pharmaceutical companies and the UK Wellcome Trust committed nearly $30 million USD to establishing the project aimed at identifying and making public an estimated 300,000 SNPs. Ultimately, they discovered 1.8 million SNPs. That information became part of the public domain, but members of the Consortium agreed that they would be able to retain downstream patent rights over innovations developed using the information revealed by the project, or over innovations developed in the course of discovery (you can learn more at snp.cshl.org).

The SNP consortium explains its willingness to privately fund the scientific work that entered the public domain rather than acquiring patent rights over the discoveries as follows:

The SNP consortium views its map as a way to make available an important, precompetitive, high-quality research tool that will spark innovative work throughout the research and industrial communities. The map will be a powerful research tool to enhance the understanding of disease processes and facilitate the discovery and development of safer and more effective medications.[13]

This is essentially the same sort of methodology used in the International HapMap Project which includes member institutes, universities, and organizations from Japan, the United States, the United Kingdom, Canada, China, and Nigeria. The project cites its goals as follows:

The International HapMap Project is a multi-country effort to identify and catalog genetic similarities and differences in human beings. Using the information in the HapMap, researchers will be able to find genes that affect health, disease, and individual responses to medications and environmental factors. The Project is a collaboration among scientists and funding agencies from [the countries listed above]. All of the information generated by the Project will be released into the public domain.[14]

The threat of patents over the domains of research encompassed by these and other similar efforts have actually prodded both private and public research to quickly develop maps, reveal their contents in the public domain, and thwart attempts at upstream patents that would likely hinder research. Another similar venture is the BiOS initiative that aims to create a public domain "toolkit" for biological and genomic innovation.[15] These are market responses to the perceived scientifically deleterious and commercially anticompetitive nature of gene patents. While these are essentially free market responses rather than governmental, some nations have elected to raise legal barriers to gene patents rather than work through existing institutions or leave it to private contracts.

National Regulation of Gene Markets

As discussed in previous chapters, certain populations make for ideal subjects in studies of genomics due to their homogeneity. This fact has led to "bio-prospecting" within such populations, often by well-financed international corporations among economically disadvantaged, indigenous populations. Presumably, the bargaining power and sophistication of the parties is not always equal. In some instances, and with increasing frequency, governments are stepping in to moderate the bargaining on behalf of their populations, developing governmentally regulated marketplaces, and attempting to equalize the bargaining power of their people.

One prime example of how a national government has cooperated with private companies and public science, and regulated the marketplace of genomic discovery in an attempt to benefit its population, is the nation of Iceland. Iceland is a prime example of a homogenous population rich with genomic relevance for scientific discovery. In 2000, the government of Iceland entered into an agreement with the company deCODE to build a national genetic database – the largest one ever conceived. The database was to take advantage of, and work in conjunction with, Iceland's already very large national health and genealogical database built up over 85 years of nationalized medicine. The partnership with deCODE was enabled by Iceland's Health Database Act, which makes publicly available the data gathered, but requires that it be de-identified so that no individual can be linked to his or her genomic information. The act enabled licensing the nation's database of genetic material to one company, in this case deCODE, for a fixed period of time. In exchange, that company was to create the database infrastructure with its own funds and in return it would be allowed to use the resource for private commercial profit. This use was further limited by certain conditions, including deCODE's bearing the costs for database development and maintenance as well as yearly fees of nearly $700,000 USD paid to Iceland "to promote health care and for research and development."[16] The fee is adjustable depending on the success of the company, and profits generated after a certain time are assessed a fee of 6 percent pre-tax, capped at $1.4 million dollars.[17]

The Icelandic agreement with deCODE is exclusive and lapses after 12 years. The exclusivity is meant to ensure greater monitoring and control by the government over the information gathered and the activities of deCODE. deCODE maintains a business presence in Iceland with a workforce of nearly 600, all of whom pay taxes in Iceland and otherwise benefit the economy. Another benefit of the partnership inures to the world at large because the data collected, even while it can be used to deCODE's profit, becomes publicly-accessible for use by researchers around the world. Even so, deCODE has been patenting discoveries as they emerge, but the profits that might accumulate from those patents will result in profit-sharing with the population as a whole through the fee system the parties established.

There is evidence that the partnership, despite some disputes and concern over privacy issues, has resulted in some rapid and significant scientific discovery. Numerous publications have come out of the partnership in reputable peer-reviewed journals. Genes associated with Alzheimer's, osteoperosis, rheumatoid arthritis, Type 2 diabetes, schizophrenia, Parkinson's, obesity, and anxiety have been discovered through the Icelandic experiment.[18]

deCODE has also formed partnerships with other companies, including Roche, a large Swiss pharmaceutical company. deCODE's partnerships have included investments from partners in the hundreds of millions of US dollars. The partnership with Roche included the provision of medicines that might be developed out of the research to the people of Iceland, a goodwill gesture meant to diffuse the appearance of bio-prospecting as exploitation.

The deCODE example offers a glimpse of how we might chart a middle ground between strong government-sponsored monopolies (patents) and a totally unfettered free market in genes. The Icelandic model involves a nationally regulated market invoking the cooperation of the population, moderated by law, and allowing for scientific exploration of a national resource. The result is designed to benefit both the public and private enterprise through encouraging science, innovation, and distributing profits among all of the parties involved. Many have since criticized the deCODE agreement, pointing out faults in the opt-out procedure (since modified) and exclusivity for licenses and profits. As an initial foray, the Icelandic model did indeed contain shortcomings that seem to have given short shrift to privacy concerns, and a potentially troubling entanglement of corporate interests with monopolistic exclusivity.[19]

For other nations concerned about exploitation of indigenous populations by gene prospecting, a modified version of the Icelandic model serves as an example of how market forces might be supervised and contracts overseen so that everyone might benefit. Bio-prospecting is taking place in locales as diverse as Sardinia and the Western Pacific, as well as among populations like the Amish, or isolated tribes in South American rainforests. The government of China recently passed a law preventing bio-prospecting within its borders without the aid and involvement of a Chinese research group.[20] Other countries such as Estonia, Mongolia, and Tonga have entered into relationships with individual corporations for bio-prospecting partnerships modeled after the Icelandic example. One large entry into this business is the Swedish company UmanGenomics which entered into an agreement with the British Medical Research Council to develop its 500,000 person genetic database.[21]

These new partnerships, and newly conceived interactions among states, universities, and corporations (including the PXE example cited in end-notes 4 and 10 of the Introduction) track in many ways new conceptions of the evolving institutions of science. In light of the unlikelihood of reverting to an idealized model of science (that may have never completely existed) involving unlimited government support, totally free and unfettered scientific inquiry, and fully cooperative "open" science, some have devised a new model that reconciles the involved parties and necessary influences of capitalists, academia, and governments. The so-called "triple helix" model lays out a foundation for science-based economic growth, involving necessary partnerships, communication, and interaction among industry, governments, and academia in what some consider to be a pragmatic, growth-based model for science and technology.[22] The Estonian, Icelandic, and British experiments in national genomics programs might all be seen as triple-helix approaches, flawed, controversial, but nonetheless honest attempts at creating synergies among the parties with an eye toward preserving benefits and rights for populations.

DNA Wants to be Free

In the world of software, a number of models now exist simultaneously. While Microsoft does not give away its operating system, prices have had to fall to compete with Open Source or freeware products. As well, quality has improved across the board as copyrighted and patented products now compete with constantly improving, lightweight Open Source products. One major difference between software and DNA, however, is that the former is inventive and would not ordinarily be the domain of scientific discovery. The objects of software do not exist freely in nature. DNA in its natural state is the object of discovery and therefore the domain of science. Science itself, as an institution dating back hundreds of years, is the original Open Source movement.

When a new particle is discovered in a particle accelerator, no one thinks of patenting it. It becomes the subject of peer-reviewed articles in top scientific journals. It helps us to understand the nature of matter, develop a greater scientific appreciation of the universe, and inspires a sense of wonder and beauty about the construction of reality at both the subatomic and cosmic levels. This is how science proceeds from discovery to discovery, usually with public investment, though sometimes in partnership with private foundations and corporations. It is part of the human endeavor and typically profit is not the motivating factor. Profit may well come out of scientific progress, and has for some time, spurred in part by intellectual property laws but not wholly dependent upon them.

The last 200 years of progress have been marked by a give and take between scientific discovery and market responses. Take the space race, for instance. Numerous spin-off technologies were commercialized from the race to land on the moon, fueled by huge public investment in what was originally a mixture of the politics of the Cold War, and pure scientific curiosity. These technologies did not pay for the race to the moon, the taxpayers did. But corporate partners in public science did profit by creating the tools and technology necessary to do the science, and by patenting and marketing things like Velcro™ and other notable inventions arising from the public space program.

For those who are wary of nationalized science programs, one alternative is a totally free market in genes – meaning one that is free of the government sponsorship of monopolies through patents. For those unwilling to experiment with totally free markets, and interested in creating greater incentives for innovation, then a modified version of the nationalized model of Iceland may make great sense. What's clear is that the present system of gene patents is burdening smaller companies and public research institutions by creating new levels of bureaucracy and expense that interfere with basic discovery. That discovery is typically undertaken by various parties with unequal access to money and other resources. DNA is a scientific domain first, like outer space or subatomic particles, and if we don't want to stifle the science, we can still encourage innovation and profits by adopting a more sensible approach and ditching the status quo. The rewards in the long run will outstrip any losses in the near term, and should include both increased innovation, and greater public understanding of the building blocks of all life.

9 | SO, WHO OWNS YOU?

SOME CONCLUSIONS ABOUT

GENES, PROPERTY, AND

PERSONHOOD

The answer to the question posed by the title of this book is clearly much more complex than our instincts would lead us to believe. We want to believe we are free, and that our bodies and every part of us is fully our own. We want to be owners of ourselves, unfettered by rights of others, obligations, or competing ownership claims over our constituent parts. But we aren't. As we have seen, there are numerous conflicting claims over ourselves, and our bodily autonomy is a myth. Not only are we restricted in what we may do with our lives (we may not kill ourselves legally), and our parts (we may not sell organs), we are also limited in the use of the *information* that lies in our personal DNA. Our genes have claims upon them, filed in the form of patents, which restrict the use to which we might want to put the essential molecules that compose us. We are partially patented, and those patents prohibit certain real-world uses of the components of our bodies. The law has enabled corporations, universities, and individuals to lay claim to parts of you. Your tissues may be used to derive profitable products, and you can sign away your rights to those products. Many do so unwittingly. This is routinely done when people become human subjects in studies. Tacked onto the consent forms of these studies are clauses that enable the researchers to use the tissues to extract DNA, and use the genes of those subjects for any purpose at any time. Are those subjects properly informed? Do they realize that parts of them might become patentable?

Arguably, few people know fully the extent of the rights they sign away when they allow the use of their genetic materials to become part of existing bio-banks, and their genes potentially patented and used for profits. Even fewer realize that even if they never participate in a research study and no tissue is removed from them, the genes they share with others may still be claimed through patents that then affect their rights to the stuff that helps make them who they are.[1]

We often own things in only limited ways. Some people lease cars and even though they might hold the title, their use of the car is restricted in a number of ways. The same is true for mortgaged properties. The books in their personal libraries are fully theirs, as are the DVDs and CDs they own, but their rights over those are also limited. They may not copy or otherwise reproduce them, and they may not perform or display them for profit without permission of the author. They own the tokens but not the types. The same is true for one fifth of our genes. We own the tokens but not the types. Yet there are clear differences between works of authorship and the complex polypeptide chains that exist in each of us and nearly every cell of our bodies.

There are a number of ways we could criticize the current practice of patenting genes. The status quo contradicts prior legal precedents and undermines legal distinctions that were once uncontroversial and universally accepted as well as useful. It may be unethical to allow ownership of something that is held in common by a community that never bargained away their rights to it. It may be inefficient for the marketplace and hinder scientific research and technological innovation. It may be immoral and akin to slavery, objectifying an essential component of each individual, and usurping our rights as persons to bodily autonomy. It may well be some, all, or none of these are true. I think that I have demonstrated a few of these, and paved the way for further investigation of other more complex, more deeply philosophical issues related to owning parts of persons. Let's consider whether and which of these possibilities is well established, and which may still need further support.

Errors in the Law

As sometimes happens, the law has attempted to deal with an object which it was ill-prepared either scientifically or philosophically to come to grips with, and ultimately it has attempted to fit square pegs into round holes. It applied the model of intellectual property law to genes with dire and confusing results. Because of this, and the fact that lawyers and judges failed to consider the long-term effects of patenting genes, as well as due to the lack of guidance by legislatures, scientists now face uncertainty, and individual rights over individual genomes have been undermined. Moreover, rights and claims of people around the world are directly altered by the actions of the US Patent and Trademark Office in setting us down the path of gene patenting. This negligence, combined with questionable application of decisions about the use of human tissues in commerce, has created the present untenable situation. There may be no going back if we don't change course now.

The law is an institution that is meant to provide predictability, stability, and in its ideal: justice. We are supposed to take comfort in the fact that laws provide guidance for behaviors, and systems of retribution and correction that balance out inequities, as well as to ensure that those who harm others are punished when caught. The law sets forth means of remunerating violations of autonomy, incursions into private property, alienation of value, breaches of private agreements, and criminal acts. The goal of the law is balancing the overall equities and helping to ensure civil order. When the law fails to achieve its purposes, there can be one of two causes and one of two cures. The cause may be either that the law incorrectly identifies the equities, or that it fails to be properly enforced. The cure may be rewriting the law according to the actual equities, or better enforcement. Not every inequity may be addressed by the law, but where the law creates institutions which it then fails to properly apply, or which are inappropriately applied to improper objects, then justice demands a cure. In some cases, the cure is altering the law, and in others, applying it more fairly through reinterpreting it.[2]

I have argued in the past for two possibilities: altering the law of intellectual property to abolish the institution of intellectual property as unnecessary and inefficient in promoting new technologies, or reforming intellectual property law to recognize that its objects are all expressions, only either *primarily* utilitarian, or *primarily* aesthetic, and that there is no bright-line dichotomy between the two along a spectrum. My argument was that computer-mediated expressions have revealed the false dichotomy in the law of intellectual property and that as new technologies emerge they will continue to pose problems for courts and innovators alike. This is because the range and nature of our expressions is increased with new technologies like computers, nanotechnology, and biotech. Things that once seemed inventive or to clearly be compositions of matter are now the result of programming, which makes these types of things seem like works of authorship. Computer software seems like both machine and work of authorship, and new programmable things will further blur this distinct as matter and life-forms become programmable at the molecular level. Genetic engineering and nanotechnology will finally undermine the distinction between "clearly" patentable inventions and copyrightable works of authorship. Life-forms and matter itself will be routinely altered, hacked, and created from scratch by programming their fundamental building blocks, and the distinction between invention and other forms of expression will be finally revealed to be untenable. The law will have to adapt.

We must recognize that the legal distinctions among types of expression are no longer workable. They fail to properly categorize when previously exclusive categories are suddenly no longer exclusive. Who is the author of genes in their natural state? Who is the inventor of DNA? This code *is* part of a larger machine, directing each of our bodies and ongoing metabolism without any intention behind it, yet creating the mechanism for our own intention. Unless we are genetically engineered, as we may become at some point, then the author and the inventor is evolution – nature itself. Christopher Columbus did not invent America, he discovered it, and Craig Venter did not invent any of the human genes that Celera discovered, though he has created new forms of life worthy of the title "invention."

If the law does not fix the error of granting patents for discoveries of the building blocks of life, and come to treat them properly as part of the scientific public domain, then further complications await. Science will be hindered, and it may yet be that our human rights and justice will suffer. Moreover, the future presents possibilities that should cause us perhaps to put the brakes on patenting life-forms in general until we develop a good theory of personhood and its relation to both our cognitive states and our genetics.

Problems of Personhood

It is the legal category "person" that most complicates granting any rights to one person over various parts of another. Persons carry obligations, rights, moral duties, and are the objects of almost all our ethical and legal considerations. There are certain agreed-upon elements of personhood that separate the legal and moral agents called "persons" from mere humans or other animals. Not all humans are conscious, nor does every human have the potential for consciousness or the necessary capacities for reason or intentionality. Dead humans, for instance, are humans but not persons. These are relatively uncontroversial distinctions. The distinctions get tougher at the other end of life – at the beginnings – where potentials and possibilities are harder to gauge, and thus our judgments are not so simple. But genes have something to do with this as they embody potentials or capacities for achieving personhood. While a dead human and a live person might share the same genes, and in the case of the live person who dies, they share identical genes, the roles of those particular genes in producing potential personhood are different. A live person's genes are responsible, if they are functioning correctly, for that person's ongoing personhood. Those same genes may become damaged fatally, resulting in the loss of actual personhood. More commonly, the capacities associated with personhood may be diminished or destroyed through some accident or degenerative condition, some of which have genetic links. If we can locate not just the qualities of personhood philosophically, but the sources of personhood genetically, then we can exercise better ethical judgment where tricky decisions might be made about potential persons.[3] In the meantime, while we have yet to reach scientific certainty about the genetic roots of our personhood, is it wise to allow property claims over its potential sources? Moreover, is it ethical? It should at least give us pause.

A number of examples help to clarify the power, and difficulty, of linking personhood to genes. The first involves a near-future scenario. Consider if we knew the genes responsible for fetal anencephaly. Children born with this defect are generally agreed to lack sight, hearing, consciousness, or the ability to feel pain. They lack the forebrain, generally considered to be the seat of consciousness. They may yet have reflex and autonomic functioning, being in some cases able to breathe and respond to touch. While these children typically die within a week of birth, withholding care in the interim is not considered to be immoral or unethical. Simply put, they are not considered persons in any normal sense of the term, and there is evidence that there is a genetic cause for their condition involving deficiencies with transcription factor TEAD2. Can we say that this genetic error, when present in the child with anencephaly, is a cause of the lack of personhood and thus the absence of certain legal and moral rights? Genes are arguably responsible in important ways for persons, even if they are not the entire *cause* of any one instance of personhood. Moreover, each of the typically accepted attributes of personhood, including consciousness, sentience, capacities for reason and intentionality, and other material attributes, is likely causally related to the proper functioning of certain genes during development, and in maintaining the relevant states over time.[4]

Not all animals are persons, and legally and morally we distinguish among humans persons and other animals. The tough cases lie closest to our branch of the evolutionary tree. Some have argued that other apes deserve treatment as persons and indeed there are different ethical requirements than for other animals when dealing with apes in research. Are the genes that are responsible for our accepting conscious, reasoning, autonomous humans as persons the same genes responsible for endowing other closely-related primates with similar capacities? The law treats persons and other humans (like dead humans, or anencephalic babies) differently, so should it treat those who share whatever genes are responsible for personhood as a class even if we were to discover that other creatures, and not just humans, shared those genes?

Of course it is not just genes that *cause* personhood, it is a combination of factors including culture and environment, but we might yet argue that certain genes are necessary but insufficient causes of personhood. If so, we might also want to consider if that genetic make-up, those genes that are causally essential to our personhood, might deserve special treatment. Should the material causes of our moral status be exempt from *any* ownership claims? The anencephaly example shows how current problems might be solved by looking at genes as a material cause of personhood and thus rights, but other scenarios argue that looking at genes can never be enough and might be just a red herring.

Other Potential Persons and Property Issues

While certain genes may be responsible for our having the attributes associated with personhood, they may only be sufficient and not necessary when looked for outside of the human race given the future potential for creating other conditions for the presence of those attributes. One thing we have learned from evolution is that genes in different species sometimes seem to find unique ways of solving the same problem. Eyes are an example. There are some forms of eyes that appear to have resulted from different evolutionary sources, some seemingly unrelated. A famous example is the octopus eye, which functions completely differently from the human eye, although the two appear externally to be similar. If evolution can form separate genetic routes to the same function of sight, could it also lead along two different paths to the problem of higher-order thought or reasoning? If so, then the mere absence of a particular gene, or set of genes, or single-nucleotide polymorphisms (SNPs), etc., that are responsible for higher-order reasoning in one species is not necessarily sufficient to claim the absence of that capacity altogether. Personhood may be linked to the presence of certain genes, but it is the *capacities* that matter in the law and in ethics. The mere absence of genes cannot cause us, without more knowledge about the particular functioning of an *individual*, to conclude anything necessarily about that individual's *person-ness*. Personhood is important, and genes relate to it, but the structure of those relations, and the universe of possible genetic forms responsible for personhood may be too great for us to form a complete theory of their interrelation any time soon.

Persons cannot ethically be property, so the decisions we make about who qualifies as a person ought not yet to be necessarily linked to such uncertain sources of potential personhood as genes. Our knowledge about genes is still too shallow to provide good guidance for any but the easiest examples (like anencephaly). Rather, we ought to concentrate on deciding which attributes of personhood matter most, and discover what beings have those attributes. Genetic studies may help but they are insufficient. We cannot own human persons, but what if we find that other sorts of things have those same attributes and yet lack the human genes responsible? Will we treat them as "ownable?" Moreover, what if we create other creatures (with software, for instance) that are capable of possessing the same attributes necessary for personhood? Will they be ownable?

This is not a mere rhetorical question. Craig Venter claims to have created a functioning organism gene by gene. This creature has been patented. The methods he used to make it are off-the-shelf genetic engineering technologies. He simply tried to figure out which genes are essential for a functioning organism, combined them using standard methods of recombinant techniques, and enclosed them in a nucleus. The result was a creature that metabolizes and functions in its environment, taking in nutrients, and *living*.[5] I have argued that genetically engineered creatures are properly patentable, being the results of human invention rather than mere discovery. Nature is revealing its toolkit for life-forms in all their diversity. This is the genius of genetic science. We are learning the relations between genes and phenotypes. With nature's toolkit, we can clearly create new things and now we can create completely new life-forms. All of which raises the ethical question: under what conditions may we *own* such new life-forms?

If we discover the genes responsible for things like consciousness and higher-order reasoning, and start splicing them into other creatures, will *persons* result? This is a sci-fi scenario raised by Michael Crichton in his book *Next*[6] and by scientists and activists who are considering "uplifting" other species by engineering them with extra genes responsible for higher-level capacities. If we do that and (for instance) engineer dogs who can reason, think, carry out intentions, and maybe even converse, then will they be persons? While they would be patentable under the analysis I have given so far, are there moral barriers to patenting such engineered persons? Are those barriers the result of the presence of those genes, or the genes plus actual capacities? Uplifted animals that might qualify for personhood are around the corner technically speaking. Starting with chimpanzees, we can look for the genetic distinctions among our species and add genes one at a time until we create a speaking, thinking chimp and interact with it as we would with other persons. Some will perhaps never accept non-human persons, either written in the code of DNA, or with software in a machine. But we should recall that prejudice caused significant historical moral lapses when we denied personhood at one time to millions of humans because of the color of their skin or due to their religion. We risk the same sort of moral lapse if we deny that personhood can exist in other media or that we can engineer it in other creatures as we learn more about its genetic sources.[7]

While at one time the law of intellectual property prohibited or was interpreted to prohibit patenting life, with the demise of that prohibition comes cause to consider the implications of allowing patents on life-forms in science fiction, or even near-future scenarios. Today's fiction is tomorrow's possibility, and the only barriers to what I have proposed are technical. They will be solved and we will have to rethink our relations to our patented creations when they too can think and question our experiments. Shall we own life in any form? Which life shall we not be able to own? When will genetic engineering enable legalized slavery? It may soon be time to revisit the generalized notion that even engineered life-forms are patentable and consider imposing some limitations on patenting them (or other creations) if they exhibit indicia of personhood.

Our Common Genetic Heritage: What Does It Mean?

All life on earth is related by birth. Some of us are more closely genetically related than others. Even the lowly fungus has at its base DNA directing its development and metabolism. The simplest forms of life, viruses, are sometimes composed of RNA rather than DNA, but viruses are not free-living. They are always parasitic on some other cell. The origin of viruses is still a mystery, but it is still likely that RNA-based viruses and DNA based organisms have some common ancestor. It will be a true scientific breakthrough if and when we discover, either on earth or on some other planet (perhaps Europa, the icy moon of Jupiter), organisms not based upon DNA. For now, all known life is related. In this sense, DNA is the common heritage of all life. While it's true that, as the Human Genome Project declared, and as the UN has acknowledged, the Human Genome is the common heritage of all humankind, why stop there?[8]

DNA is the common heritage of *all known life*. We are distant cousins of the other apes and all primates are distant cousins of the mouse, and so on. The forces that caused us to all diverge, and for life to choose different paths to survive, were beyond our control until now. Accident and happenstance caused some evolutionary choices to survive and others to go extinct, some to become dominant and others to become subjugated. Chance enabled some to become intelligent while others remain blissfully ignorant. Now, we can direct these forces to a degree. Science is fulfilling its general tendency to give us greater understanding, prediction, and now – control. As we learn more about the mechanisms of evolution and the relations of genes to phenotypes, we are gaining power over life itself. It's a rather awesome power, and one that we will need to direct with extremely good judgment. We will be able to cure diseases, to provide bountiful resources, to save species from extinction (perhaps even our own) and to alter the effects of nature's chance and happenstance. This new knowledge gives us an equally awesome responsibility. Our horizon for prediction and control is still very short. The nature of genomes is that they are complex, having evolved over billions of years, and we learn unpredicted things on a daily basis about DNA and its relations to organisms and their environments. Our choices in altering life-forms may effect life on earth in perpetuity, so we had best tread carefully in order to avoid disasters.

One thing about life is that it is stubborn. It goes on despite disasters. It has lasted through ice ages and meteor impacts. It will likely outlast us as a species. In the meantime, we should respect the power of DNA and the forces of evolution, and use it wisely. The benefits we stand to gain are enormous. We could wipe out diseases, and benefit both humanity and the planet by eliminating scarcity, developing cleaner fuels, and producing abundant food. We owe these possibilities to that double helix that composes and directs every free-living thing. We might ask ourselves, given these potential benefits, given all the promise that the new genetic tech-nologies hold, should we allow greed and commerce to interfere with achieving the scientific and technical potentials we envision? We have learned in the past that resources may be squandered and may be ruined or eliminated by market forces unchecked by legal, moral, or ethical con-siderations. It is time for us to think about whether and how we can appro-priately regulate this common resource to avoid potential disasters and to best promote some notion of collective and individual justice. Until we learn more about DNA, and can make better, more informed decisions into the distant horizon as to its use and alteration, we should, for both practical and ethical reasons, treat all DNA as part of a common heritage, not just of humankind, but of all life on this planet. If we are to be good stewards of this knowledge, and to use it wisely to promote both human and plane-tary health, we should expect that research on DNA be done in the open, through traditional channels of open science, and released into the public domain.

Your Genome/Our Genome

Even while we are inextricably linked to each other and to all known life through DNA, we are also undeniably individuals with unique personal genomes. We are entering an age of "personal genomics" in which the information we will have access to regarding our individual genomes will vastly expand. This information can liberate us, or it could help enslave us. It can liberate us by allowing us to make much better decisions about our diets, our health care choices, our reproductive choices, and how we choose to go about our daily lives. It can give us information that will enable us to take charge of our personal futures and remove a fair amount of doubt and chance from our life-plans. Of course, balancing freedom with knowl-edge that carries the potential to remove much doubt is a challenge, but it's not an unfamiliar one. Health care in general has improved to enable us to make more careful predictions about risks, and to make choices with greater information. In our individual hands, knowledge about our per-sonal genomes can be liberating, but in the hands of others it may help us lose liberties.

Companies like 23andMe, Inc., who promise to give us detailed informa-tion about our individual genomes, will spring up left and right in the next few decades. This company offers to scan your genome for a mere $1,000. It looks for the presence of SNPs associated with various health disorders and infirmities, and provides information that helps customers to evaluate their chances of suffering various diseases known to be genetically-linked. This sort of information can be a boon to customers if they are properly informed, but that depends upon so much. It depends on the current state of the art and the level of scientific certainty about genetically-linked health and disease traits. It depends also upon the level of sophistication of the customers and their abilities to comprehend the choices that are implied by statistical chances of incurring diseases. It also depends upon privacy. This is a case where too much knowledge may be dangerous in ways that too little knowledge is not . . . yet.

Useful scientific data has emerged from the various "mapping" projects seeking to reveal the intricacies of genomes and phenotypes. We are learning how we are built from the molecule on up. Donors to these projects have greatly aided our collective scientific advance and given us important tools to help develop treatments and possible cures for diseases. But these donors are generally anonymous. While some have revealed their genomes with intimate detail (e.g. Jim Watson and Craig Venter), others have not done so and probably with good reason. In a future that promises complete genomic transparency we will have to consider the degree to which we wish to maintain control over our individual genomic data, and whether and how we might be able to exert that control. Right now, the means of doing so is very limited both legally and practically. Just as you are not the owner of tissue extracted from you for either medical or research purposes, you are not the legal owner of any part of you that is not attached to your body. The legal status of your tissues once removed is currently only defined by contract, and that only applies to tissues you agree to part with. So far, your ownership of your tissues removed during medical and research procedures depends upon the clinical-ethical notion that human subjects must give "informed consent" to have their tissues used. But most human subjects in clinical medical contexts probably cannot fully appreciate the long-term consequences of agreeing to allow their genes to be stored and used. This was the case in *Moore*, the case involving the patenting of products derived from Mr Moore's spleen cells. Few laypeople understand the relation of genes to their bodies, much less the potential commercial and scientific uses of their DNA in the future.[9]

It is not merely that laypeople lack scientific knowledge about genes that prevents them from giving truly informed consent, but it is also the fact that the potential future uses of genes are often unknown even to the scientists extracting those tissues. When tissues make their way into bio-banks, the "donor" loses all legal claims unless specifically retained by contract, and few scientists would voluntarily draft an informed consent form that would hamper his or her future uses of the tissues extracted. Greed may not be the motivating factor, it may well just be good scientific sense. Tissues in bio-banks may have currently unknown future scientific uses. In fact, samples in existing bio-banks for which broad consent forms were signed in the past, before any potential genomic or genetic use for the tissues was conceived, are now ripe for the picking for genomic studies.

If we create a marketplace in which tissue samples are given more frequently, yet with no greater education of donors or choices as to the use of those samples, then individuals will be bargaining away future claims to their tissues without fully appreciating the consequences. In the case of private companies like 23andMe, we should be wary that customers are not granting future license to utilize genes for profit without adequate knowledge of the consequences, nor given their limited ability to bargain for greater reward. Your $1,000 fee might return that investment for that gene scanning company a hundredfold if that company becomes able to patent some discovery based upon the sample you provided. You as a consumer ought to be able to secure greater bargaining leverage in such a deal. We need more educated consumers, patients, and donors, and some ethical acknowledgment on the part of potential profit-makers in the marketplace that they ought to consider giving back to individuals, as well as to humanity as a whole, our fair share.

But there is more at stake. Beyond merely fair shares in potential future profits, and some leveling of the playing field through greater awareness and education, we need to enter into some real public discussion about privacy and property concerns regarding genes. As more of our individual genomes become obtainable, either through private commerce, public bio-banks, clinical practice, and research, we are spreading information about ourselves that we would generally consider to be private. Your propensity for diabetes, your likelihood for alcoholism, your risk for developing Alzheimer's, and so on, are all things that you would probably wish to know before anyone else, and which you would rather be in charge of either keeping secret or divulging as you see fit. As anyone who has seen the movie *Gattaca* knows, this sort of information will be extremely valuable to others, including to insurance companies, governments, employers, and potential mates. Yet typically we submit to tissue sampling through blood draws and other medical procedures without any consideration of where those samples might end up. Routinely, subjects take part in clinical trials with little-to-no realization as to the potential uses to which their tissues might be put, and just as routinely, consent forms include a clause indicating that the samples might be kept for future genetic studies. Given the lack of general knowledge by the public about DNA and its functioning, much less its potential profitable uses, we need to consider balancing the scales a bit and creating greater positive safeguards for genetic privacy.[10]

The United Kingdom and Estonia offer us two different scenarios of the future of genetic databases. Estonia recently enacted a national database standard that requires citizens to "opt-in," citing Icelandic citizens' reactions to the agreement of that government with deCODE, Inc. that required an explicit and complicated opt-out. The U.K. now has *de facto* the world's largest genetic database, as it already compiles and keeps genetic samples gathered from all crime scenes. The samples are from both victims and criminals, and the database includes more than three million individual samples, including half a million from children under 16 years old. Needless to say, these samples have been mostly obtained without consent and there are significant concerns about privacy. How will they be used? Can the government, which is the proprietor of those databases, use them to profile populations or individuals? Can that information be used to deny medical coverage under the UK's system of socialized medicine to someone, for instance, with the genetic propensity for lung cancer who chooses to continue to smoke? If we discover a genetic link for certain criminal propensities, can that genetic information be used to profile and sequester people who might be *future* offenders (as in the movie *Minority Report*, but using genes rather than "precognition")?[11]

If we wish to avoid nightmare sci-fi scenarios, we need to consider creating greater personal control over not just our tissue samples, but also perhaps our individual genomes . . . their types, not just the tokens. Clearly there is no natural or brute fact claim over these things, as our genetic material routinely sloughs off our bodies and we retain no ability to control it. This was never an issue for privacy in a pre-genetic screening world. But now it is a significant issue with considerable privacy implications. Anyone could technically find your genes and link them to you, and soon that will give others great power over you. To control this, should we wish to, we would need to enact positive laws that *create new rights* over our individual genes. Just as we have legally created new zones of privacy over financial and medical data, we could develop legal schemes that protect one's individual rights over one's individual genome. It is likely that such a scheme would have widespread public support. While potential profiteers of the human genome might object, scientists and researchers could embrace this and still pursue their research.

As stakeholders in the future use of their individual DNA, human subjects, patients, and others who donate tissue might actually be encouraged to cooperate with research. They might well have greater confidence in the potential scientific use of their genes, and greater legal capabilities to bargain over those uses, while still preserving some individual rights and control in the future. Scientists could benefit by having better informed, more willing subjects, and by cutting down on the uncertainty associated with the current patent regime. The future risks of current research could be cut down. Cases like *Moore* would be fewer and further between if individuals were given greater knowledge and control over the uses of their genes, and future concerns of privacy and intrusion would be eliminated if anticipated in private contracts between freely bargaining parties. Creating a legally recognized individual right over one's individual genome need not preclude the public use of our common genome for scientific purposes either. Most of our genome is shared, and that part may not be laid claim to by anyone in particular if we recognize the domain as a commons. As a commonly held resource, it may be used for the public good as long as it isn't "wasted" or destroyed. But the portions that are *unique* to us as individuals could be set aside from public use, while still freely bargained over by the "possessor" with the scientific community, governments, or the public at large. Such a system would accommodate future privacy concerns and create a marketplace with more equality for the bargaining parties. It might even be more just if we decide that people ought to have greater control over the products of their bodies even if there is no *natural* right over them. We have created rights before, including (broadly speaking) modern notions of legal privacy that never existed until recently and that we now take for granted. Privacy, as a matter of brute fact, does not exist in any natural sense except by secret-keeping, although zones of privacy have been legally created and expanded over time. It might well be time to extend these legal guarantees given new genetic technologies.[12]

Future Issues: Where Do We Go from Here?

I have laid out some of the possible scenarios that we face given both current practices and future technological trends. We are heading toward an eventual complete understanding of the human genome and its role and relations evolutionarily to genomes of other species. This understanding will reveal nature's vast toolkit of genes, SNPs, copy-number variants, and other modes of passing on traits, both successful and debilitating. This knowledge will potentially liberate us from the cruel vagaries of evolution and chance, and allow us to overcome our limitations and diseases. This future is presently on the verge of a bottleneck. As the human genome became completely mapped, some have staked out their private claims, and the next decade or so will be muddled in litigation and slowed investigation while these claims get sorted out.

I have made a number of suggestions as to how we should proceed, addressing some philosophical and legal questions that can and should be resolved now, but leaving open some others that will require future scrutiny. We can and should abort the present process of granting gene patents over non-engineered genes. This is because not only are these legally unpatentable under any rational interpretation of intellectual property law, but genes are ethically *un-ownable* by any one party as they are a "commons," unencloseable, and the duty of all to maintain and hold. Many human genes may also relate in necessary, though as yet poorly understood, ways with our moral status as persons. Moreover, our concerns over privacy ought to lead us to create new, positive protections for individuals over their individual genomes. We should recognize an individual right and duty to be our own proprietors of our individual genetic identities, even as we recognize the common rights and duties we share over our collective genetic identity as members of the same species.

Science demands these reforms too, as public investment in research into the basis of our common heritage is being used to enclose resources that ought not to be enclosed. This is not just an ethical problem, but also a practical one that chills future research. With the tremendous expense and burden of patent litigation, basic researchers must tread carefully and sort out the likelihood of unintentionally stepping on patent claims before pursuing research on parts of the genome. This expense and burden may be too great in some instances to risk starting the research. The first to file a claim gets the patent regardless of who may have discovered or worked on the gene first, and one might have wasted limited resources in studying a gene or a SNP that then becomes off-limits when another party patents it. Our individuality and our genes, as well as these other legal, practical, and philosophical concerns, may be reasons enough to hold our genes off-limits to ownership. Our privacy concerns as well ought to lead us to develop new conceptions of individual proprietorship over the genetic bases for our individuality.

There are many more issues only touched on but unquestionably important and worthy of deeper investigation. Our law and ethics have for some time focused upon notions of *personhood* in affording rights, duties, and legal status. There is some genetic link between the capacities we associate with personhood and legal or moral status. We need to account for the links between useful biological facts and social facts. Our decisions about how to treat new and emerging potential persons depend in no small part on our definitions of what personhood includes, and which genes are responsible for its presence in a living human being. This is a philosophical investigation that goes far beyond the scope of this book and would have to encompass legal theory, ethics, cognitive science, and a host of other disciplines. While acknowledging that this important issue informs further our treatment of genes in the law, it is not dispositive of the issue of whether genes ought to be owned or to what extent.

We have answered enough for now to say with clarity that something is wrong. We have overstepped the bounds not only of the law of patent, but also some basic ethical facts. These facts are grounded and recognized in institutions that treat certain resources as beyond individual ownership and as belonging to the public at large – useable only for the public good. Until now, both the institutions of science and the law have recognized our common ownership of these sorts of resources and legally, ethically, and practically, we have all benefited from keeping them in the public domain. Gene patents are an anomaly. Their patenting is now a real threat both to science and to ethical norms that have guided our laws and directed our actions regarding the commons for centuries. It is time to stop. We must call on our leaders to recognize that our common human heritage cannot be chopped up, enclosed, and apportioned for profit, but must be put to public, scientific, and technical use without the hindrance of greed. It is ours, not theirs, and we should take charge of it again. Both science and ethics demand it.

NOTES

Introduction

1   Shreeve, J 2004, *The Genome War*, Ballantine Books, New York, p. 37.
2   Redon, et al. 2006, "Global variation in copy number in the human genome," *Nature*, November 23, pp. 444–54.
3   Gross, M 2005, "Human genome carve-up continues," *Current Biology*, vol. 15, no. 22.
4   Terry, PF 2003, "PXE International: harnessing international property law for benefit sharing," in Knoppers BM (ed.) *Populations and Genetics: Legal and Socio-Ethical Perspectives*, 2003, Martinus Nijhoff Publishers, Leiden, Netherlands, p. 381.
5   Montagu, A 1971, *The Elephant Man: A Study in Human Dignity*, E. P. Dutton, New York.
6   Ghatenekar, SD & Mandar, S Ghatenekar, SM 1999, "Bio-prospecting or bio-piracy?" *Express India*, Feb. 8.
7   Laird, S &Wynberg, R 2007, "Bioprospecting: securing a piece of the pie," *World Conservation*, pp. 28–9, cmsdata.iucn.org/downloads/24_world_conservation_2008_01.pdf (accessed February 24, 2008).
8   "Canavan Foundation Joint Press Release," Sept. 29, 2003, www.canavan foundation.org/news/09-03_miami.php (accessed October 16, 2006)
9   Suderland, T et al. "The Bioresources Development & Conservation Programme – Camaroon" at Earthwatch Institute, Limbe Conference, www.earthwatch.org
10 See Terry, PF 2003.
11 Columbia Pictures Corp. 1997, Directed by Andrew Niccol.
12 Moor, JH 1999, "Using genetic information while protecting the privacy of the soul," *Ethics and Information Technology*, vol. 1, pp. 257–63.
13 Koepsell, D 2000, *The Ontology of Cyberspace: Law, Philosophy, and the Future of Intellectual Property*, Open Court, Chicago, IL.

Chapter 1

1 Berry, RM 2003, "Genetic information and research: emerging legal issues," *Healthcare Ethics Committee Forum*, vol. 15, pp. 70–99.

2 Lenoir, N 2003, "Patentability of life and ethics" in *C.R. Biologies*, vol. 326, pp. 1127–34, p. 1129 (describes National Institutes of Health head, Bernadine Healy, permitting Craig Venter's company Celera, Inc. patenting genes discovered through its private work on the HGP); Koepsell D 2007, "Preliminary Questions" in *Journal of Evolution and Technology*, Vol. 16, Issue 1, June 2007, pp. 151–9.

3 Askland, A 2003, "Patenting genes: a fast and furious primer," *International Journal of Applied Philosophy*, vol. 17, pp. 267–75.

4 McCain, L 2002, "Informing technology policy decisions: the U.S. Human Genome Project's Legal and Social Implications Programs as a critical case," *Technology in Society*, vol. 24, pp. 111–32.

5 At least there are no such natural rights to anything more than their tokens. For example, the token of *Moby Dick* is the physical book containing the printed words depicting the story. The *type* is the universal form, reproduced in each individual book. The type remains the same no matter the particular form of its reproduction in a particular token.

6 Singer, M & Berg, P 1991, *Genes and Genomes*, University Science Books, Mill Valley, CA, pp. 131–2.

7 *Diamond v. Chakrabarty*, 447 U.S. 303 (1980), *Moore v. Regents of the University of California*, 51 Cal. 3d. 120 (1990).

8 Chakrabarty, AM 2003, "Environmental biotechnology in the postgenomics era," *Biotechnology Advances*, vol. 22, pp. 3–8.

9 Gostin, LO & Hodge, JG Jr. 1999, "Genetic privacy and the law: an end to genetics exceptionalism," *Jurimetrics*, vol. 40, Fall, p. 21.

10 Cunningham, PC 2003, "Is it right or is it useful? Patenting of the human gene, Lockean property rights, and the erosion of the Imago Dei," *Ethics and Medicine*, vol. 19, pp. 85–98.

11 Searle, J 1997, *The Construction of Social Reality*, Free Press, New York.

12 See generally, Koepsell, D 2000 *The Ontology of Cyberspace: Law, Philosophy, and the Future of Intellectual Property*, Open Court, Chicago, IL.

13 Wheale, PR & McNally, R 2003, "A synoptic survey of the bioethics of human genome research," *International Journal of Biotechnology*, vol. 5, pp. 21–37.

14 As Open Source guru Stewart Brand famously said, "information wants to be free" in *Whole Earth Review*, May 1985, p. 49.

15 Winickoff, DE & Neumann, LB 2005, "Towards a social contract for genomics: property and the public in the 'biotrust' model," *Genomics, Society and Policy*, vol. 1, no. 3, pp. 8–21.

16   Hoedemaekers, R & Dekkers, W 2001, "Is there a unique moral status of human DNA that prevents patenting?" *Kennedy Institute of Ethics Journal*, vol. 11, pp. 359–86.

17   Witek, R 2005, "Ethics and patentability in biotechnology," *Science and Engineering Ethics*, vol. 11, pp. 105–11.

18   Compare with Arthur Caplan who argues that there's nothing special about the human genome and thus it should be patentable. Unfortunately he and other commentators who make this argument ignore the fact that ordinarily, discoveries are not afforded patent protection – only inventions are. He is right that the human genome is not particularly special, but his conclusion is not informed by a good understanding of intellectual property law. Caplan, A 1998 "What's so special about the human genome?" *Cambridge Quarterly of Healthcare Ethics*, vol. 7, pp. 422–4.

19   Beauchamp, TL & Walters, L 1982, *Contemporary Issues in Bioethics* (3rd edn.), Wadsworth Publishing Co., Belmont, CA, pp. 12–25 (discussing various ethical theories).

20   Guenin, LM 2003, "Dialogue concerning natural appropriation," *Synthese*, vol. 136, pp. 321–36.

Chapter 2

1   Koepsell, D 2007, "Ethics and ontology: a new synthesis," *Metaphysica*, vol. 8, no. 2, October, pp. 20–27.

2   Reinach, A 1983, *The Apriori Foundations of the Civil Law*, trans. John F. Crosby, reprinted in *Aletheia*, vol. III, pp. 1–142.

3   Reinach, A 1983, pp. 2–4.

4   Koepsell, D 2000, *The Ontology of Cyberspace: Philosophy, Law, and the Future of Intellectual Property*, Open Court, Chicago, IL, p. 130.

5   Reinach, A 1983, pp. 53–4.

6   Searle, J 1997, *The Construction of Social Reality*, Free Press, New York (describing the relations of "brute facts," intentionality, and "social reality").

Chapter 3

1   Singer M & Berg P 1991, *Genes and Genomes*, University Science Books, Mill Valley, CA, pp. 17–18.

2   Piel, G 2001, *The Age of Science*, Basic Books, New York, pp. 243–4.

3   www.stat.washington.edu/thompson/Genetics/2.4_experiments.html (accessed January 16, 2008).

174   NOTES

4   Griffiths AJF et al. 2000, *An Introduction to Genetic Analysis* (7th edn.), WH Freeman & Co, New York.

5   Somatic cells are those cells that are part of the body, but not gametes. Gametes are reproductive cells like sperm or eggs.

6   Piel, G 2001, pp. 251–2.

7   Piel, G 2001, pp. 251–2.

8   Ridley, M 1996, *Evolution* (2nd edn.), Blackwell Science, Oxford, pp. 9–19.

9   A phage is a virus that is parasitic of bacteria. Phages infect bacteria with their own genes, taking over the machinery of the bacterium in order to reproduce themselves.

10   Piel, G 2001, pp. 256–7.

11   Watson, J 1980, *The Double Helix: A Personal Account of the Discovery of the Structure of DNA* (2nd edn.), Atheneum, New York.

12   Watson, J 1980.

13   "The Meselson-Stahl Experiment," www.highered.mcgraw-hill.com/olc/dl/120076/bio.swf (accessed March 26, 2008).

14   Piel, G 2001, pp. 261–7.

15   Singer, M & Berg, P 1991, *Genes and Genomes*, University Science Books, Mill Valley, CA, pp. 66–7.

16   www.sickle.bwh.haravard.edu/ingram.html (accessed March 16, 2008).

17   Yanofsky, C, Carlton, BC, Guest, JR, et al. 1964, "On the colinearity of gene structure and protein structure" in *Proceedings of the National Academy of Sciences*, vol. 51, no. 2, p. 266.

18   Piel, G 2001, pp. 261–70.

19   British mathematician Alan Turing's vision of an idealized computing machine, capable of computing any information, was of a single tape, encoded with binary information, which moves forward or back according to its instructions relative to some reading mechanism. Human DNA is a 3 billion base pair long "tape" with instructions read by numerous other mechanisms, all themselves encoded for and instructed for also by the same DNA. All of the feedback mechanisms involved with DNA are much more complicated than Turing's idealized machine.

20   Ridley, M 1996, pp. 22–6.

21   Britannica Online, "Jacques Monod," www.brittanica.com/eb/article-9053397/Jacques-Monod (accessed March 20, 2008).

22   www.geneontology.org

23   www.hopkinsmedicine.org/press/2002/November/epigenetics.htm (accessed March 13, 2008).

Chapter 4

1   science.jrank.org/pages/5047/Parthenogenesis-Sexual-vs-non-sexual-reproduction.html (accessed July 2, 2007).

2   It is worth noting that, partly in protest to efforts to patent life-form, Jeremy Rifkin and Stuart Newman sought a patent on a human-chimp "chimera" incorporating a mixture of genes of each related species. The patent application was denied because the result was "too human." Weiss R 2005, "U.S. denies patent for a too-human hybrid: scientist sought legal precedent to keep others from profiting from similar 'inventions'," *Washington Post*, Feb. 13, p. A03.

3   Cowen, R 2000, *History of Life* (3rd edn.), Blackwell Science, Inc., Malden, Mass., p. 43.

4   Paulson T, 2005, "Chimp, human DNA comparison finds vast similarities, key differences", *Seattle Post-Intelligencer*, Sept. 1, "local" section, p. 1, citing *Nature* study.

5   Yale University 2004, "Most recent common ancestor of all living humans surprisingly recent," *Science Daily*, 30 September. www.sciencedaily.com/releases/2004/09/040930122428.htm (accessed March 22, 2008).

6   Shreeve, J 2004, *The Genome War*, Ballantine Books, New York.

7   De Queiroz, K 2005, "Ernst Mayr and the modern concept of species," *Proceedings of the National Academy of Sciences*, vol. 102, Suppl. 1, pp. 6600–607.

8   Pinker, S 2008, "The moral instinct," *New York Times*, January 13.

9   "'Junk' DNA now looks like powerful regulator, researcher finds," physorg.com, Apr. 23, 2007, www.physorg.com/news96567418.html (accessed March 12, 2008).

10 Owen, J 2006, "DNA varies more widely from person to person, genetic maps reveal," *National Geographic News*, November 22.

11 Dawkins, R 1995, *River out of Eden*, Basic Books, New York.

12 Strawson, PF 1959, *Individuals*, Methuen, London (for an excellent discussion of individuals).

13 The caveat "so far" is used to admit that we must recognize that personhood may at some point be recognized in non-human objects capable of the full range of other necessary features of personhood. At this point, however, personhood has only been ascribed to certain human individuals with certain necessary and sufficient conditions and features.

Chapter 5

1   Brief for Petitioner, p. 13, *Diamond v. Chakrabarty*, No. 79–136, 1980 WL 339757 (U.S. Jan. 4, 1980); Koepsell D 2007, "3 Billion Little Pieces: How Much of You do You Own?" *SciTech Lawyer*, Vol. 3, No. 4, pp. 8–11.

2   Bugos, GE & Kevles, DJ 1992, *Plants as Intellectual Property: American Practice, Law, and Policy in World Context*, University of Chicago Press, Chicago, IL.

3   *In re Bergy*, 563 F.2d 1031, 1032 (C.C.P.A. 1977); *In re Chakrabarty*, 571 F.2d 40, 42 (C.C.P.A. 1978).

4   *Bergy* at p. 1033.

5   *In re Mancy*, 499 F.2d 1289, 1294 (C.C.P.A. 1974).

6   *Bergy* at p. 1036.

7   54 F.2d 400 (D. Del. 1931).

8   *Bergy* at p. 1038.

9   *Chakrabarty* at p. 44.

10 2 U.S.P.Q2d (BNA) 1425, 1426 (Bd. Pat. App. & Inter., 1987).

11 "Animals – Patentability", 1077 Off. Gaz Pat. Office 18, 24 (Apr. 21, 1987).

12 US Patent 4,736,866 granted to Harvard College claiming "a transgenic non-human mammal whose germ cells and somatic cells contain a re-combinant activated oncogene sequence introduced into said mammal . . ."

13 Patents and the Constitution: Transgenic Animals: Hearing on Supplemental Appropriations Act Before the House Subcomm. On Courts, Civil Liberties, and the Admin. Of Justice, 100th Cong. 2 (1987), p. 25.

14 H.R. 3119 (100th Cong.).

15 S. 2111 (100th Cong.)

16 S. 387 (103d Cong.), 138 Cong. Rec. 9591 (1992).

17 Utility and Examination Guidelines, 66 Fed. Reg. 1092, p. 1093 (Jan. 5, 2001).

18 Shreeve, J 2004, *The Genome War*, Ballantine Books, New York.

19 Shreeve, J 2004.

20 See, for example, *Haelen Laboratories Inc., v. Topps*, 202 F.2d 866 (2d Cir. 1953).

Chapter 6

1   Choate, RA, Francis, WH, & Collins, RC 1987, *Patent Law: Case & Materials*, West Publishing Co., MN, pp. 4–5.

2   For more depth on the history of intellectual property laws, see Koepsell, D 2000, *The Ontology of Cyberspace: Philosophy, Law, and the Future of Intellec-tual Property*, Open Court, Chicago, IL, ch. 4.

3   Choate, RA, Francis, WH, & Collins, RC 1987, pp. 62–6.

4   See, for example, Gordon, WJ 1993 "A property right in self-expression: equal-ity and individualism in the natural law of intellectual property," *Yale Law Journal*, vol. 102, no. 7 (May), pp. 1533–1609.

5   Hughes, J 1988, "The philosophy of intellectual property," *Georgetown Law Journal*, vol. 77, p. 287.

6   Principally spurred on by passage of the Bayh–Dole Act in the US in 1980, which gave to university scientists never-before available rights in profits and patents from government-sponsored and funded research. See Branscomb LM, Kodama F, & Florida RL1999, *Industrializing Knowledge*, MIT Press, Cambridge, MA.

7   Koepsell, D 2000, p. 130.
8   This statement has traditionally been ascribed to Stewart Brand, founder
    of the Whole Earth Catalog, and written first in an issue of the *Whole
    Earth Review* in 1984.
9   Reinach, A 1983, *The Apriori Foundations of the Civil Law*, trans. John F.
    Crosby, reprinted in *Aletheia*, vol. III, pp. 4–5, 53–4.
10 450 U.S. 175 (1981).

Chapter 7

1   Gargano, B 2005, "The quagmire of DNA patents: are DNA sequences more
    than chemical compositions of matter," *Syracuse Science and Technology Law
    Reporter*, Rep. 3, 5.
2   Kane, EM 2004, "Splitting the gene: DNA patents and the genetic code," *Ten-
    nessee Law Review,* vol. 71, p. 707.
3   Chander, A & Sunder, M 2004, "The romance of the public domain,"
    California Law Review, vol. 92, pp. 1331–74.
4   Compare with Spinello, RA 2004, "Property rights in genetic information,"
    Ethics and Information Technology, vol. 6, pp. 29–42. (Discusses utilitarian
    arguments opposing "upstream" property rights in genes.)
5   Dickenson, D 2004, "Consent, commodification, and benefit sharing in genetic
    research," *Developing World Bioethics*, vol. 4, no. 2, pp. 109–24.
6   Wilson, SR 2004, "Copyright protection for DNA sequences: can the biotech
    industry harmonize science with song?" *Jurimetrics*, vol. 44, pp. 409–63.
7   Neeson, JM 1996, *Commoners: Common Right, Enclosure, and Social
    change in England, 1700–1820*, Cambridge University Press, Cambridge;
    Benkler, Y 2003, "The political economy of commons," *Upgrade*, vol. IV,
    no. 3, pp. 6–9. Hardin's term comes from an article he published in *Science*
    in 1968 describing the dilemma which is now an icon in socio-political
    theory.
8   Ostrom, E 1990, *Governing the Commons*, Cambridge University Press,
    Cambridge.
9   Zhang, S 2004, "Proposing resolutions to the insufficient gene patent system,"
    *Santa Clara Computer and High Technology Law Journal & High Tech Law
    Institute Publications*, vol. 20, pp. 1139–50. (Discusses problems and potential
    solutions for the gene patenting system.)
10 Devil's Tower is an iconic, natural landmark in South Dakota. It is perhaps
    best known for its famous appearance in the movie *Close Encounters of the
    Third Kind*, directed by Steven Spielberg (1977).
11 Doremus, H 1999, "Nature, knowledge, and profit: the Yellowstone bio-
    prospecting controversy and the core purposes of America's national parks,"

Ecology Law Quarterly, vol. 26. (Suggests the category of "commons" for DNA, as have many others, but without the analysis offered above about the nature of the commons. Doremus also suggests that there are matters of social justice involved.)

Chapter 8

1   Porter, R 2000, *The Creation of the Modern World*, W.W. Norton & Co., NewYork, pp. 145–6.
2   See Blanpied WA, 1998 "Inventing US science policy," *Physics Today*, Feb., pp. 34–40, explaining the divergence of the post-WWII system of US science funding from the idealized vision of Vannevar Bush, and pointing out its roots in the Cold War.
3   Mason, SF 1962, *A History of the Sciences*, Collier Books, New York, pp. 591–2.
4   "What is a superconducting supercollider?" BBC Online, July 5, 2004, www.bbc.co.uk/dna/h2g2/A2754623 (accessed December 15, 2007).
5   35 U.S.C. § 200–12.
6   See, for example, Greenberg, D 2007, *Science for Sale*, Chicago: University of Chicago Press, Chicago.
7   See also Venter, JC 2007, *A Life Decoded*, Viking, NewYork.
8   Lovgren, S 2005, "One-fifth of human genes have been patented, study reveals," *National Geographic News*, October 13.
9   *NIE Glossary*, Ronald Coase Institute, www.coase.org/nieglossary (accessed March 12, 2008).
10   Moore, A 2000, "Owning genetic information and gene enhancement techniques: why privacy and property rights may undermine social control of the human genome," *Bioethics*, vol. 14, no. 2, pp. 97–119. (Argues a Lockean perspective in individual gene ownership.)
11   GNU stands for GNU is Not Unix. It's a recursive acronym and could only have emerged from a place like MIT.
12   www.brainyquote.com/quotes/authors/r/richard_stallman.html   (accessed March 14, 2008).
13   Human Genome Project Information, SNP Fact Sheet, www.ornl.gov/sci/techresources/Human_Genome/faq/snps.shtml (accessed February 21, 2008).
14   "About the HapMap," www.hapmap.org/thehapmap.html.en (accessed February 21, 2008).
15   The BiOS Initiative explains: "We are adapting licensing and distributive collaboration aspects of the open source movement to enhance transparency, accessibility, and capability to use patented technology, public domain sci-

ences know-how and materials. Biological Open Source (BiOS) is focused on the enablement of creative people everywhere." See www.bios.net

16   Agreement Relating to the Issue of an Operating License for the Creation and Operation of a Health Sector Database, Jan 21, 2000, www.raduneyti.is/interpro/htr.nsf/Files/Aggreement/Sfile/AGREEMENT-english.pdf (accessed December 15, 2007).

17   Potts J 2002, "At least give the natives glass beads: an examination of the bargain made between Iceland and decode genetics with implications for global bioprospecting," *Virginia Journal of Law and Technology*, vol. 7, no. 8.

18   See also Palsson, G & Rabinow, P 2001, "The Icelandic genome debate," *Trends in Biotechnology*, vol. 19, no. 5, pp. 166–71; Barker, JH 2003, "Common-pool resources and population genomics in Iceland, Estonia, and Tonga," *Medicine, Health Care and Philosophy*, vol. 6, pp. 133–44.

19   Koay, PP 2004 "An Icelandic (ad)venture: new research? New subjects? New ethics?" in Roelcke, V and Maio, G 2004, *Twentieth Century Ethics of Human Subjects Research: Historical Perspectives*, Franz Steiner Verlag, Stuttgart.

20   See usembassy-china.org.cn/sandt/generesourcesreg10-98.html (accessed Feb. 21, 2008).

21   See Godard, B et. al 2004, "Strategies for Consulting with the Community," *Science and Engineering Ethics*, vol. 10, pp. 457–77; Sutrop, M & Simm, K, "The Estonian healthcare system and the genetic database project, from limited resources to big hopes," *Cambridge Quarterly of Healthcare Ethics*, vol. 13, pp. 254–63.

22   Leydesdorff, L & Etzkowitz, H 1998, "The triple helix as a model for innovation studies (Conference Report)," *Science & Public Policy*, vol. 25, no. 3, pp. 195–203.

Chapter 9

1   Levine, RJ 1981, *Ethics and Regulation of Clinical Research* (2nd edn.), Yale University Press, New Haven, CT, pp. 95–8 (for a basic description of the requirements of informed consent).

2   Berry, RM 2003, "Genetic information and research: emerging legal issues," *Healthcare Ethics Forum*, vol. 15, no.1, pp. 70–99. (Surveys a range of legal issues including those we have discussed in this book.)

3   Flowers, EB 1998, "The ethics and economics of patenting the human genome," *Journal of Business Ethics*, vol. 17, pp. 1737–45. (Discusses issues of human dignity involved in gene patents.)

4   Wilson, EO 1998, *Consilience*, Alfred P. Knopf, Inc., New York, pp. 140–1. (Regarding interaction of genes, environment, and individual traits.)

5   Venter, JC 2007, *A Life Decoded*, Viking, New York, pp. 350–7.

6   Crichton, M. 2006, *Next*, HarperCollins, New York.

7   Heller, JC 1998, "Human genome research and the challenge of contingent future persons: toward an impersonal theocentric approach to value," *Bioethics*, vol. 12, no. 2, pp. 173–6. (Describes concerns discussed above and considering them from a theistic perspective.)

8   Byk, C 1998, "A map to a new treasure island: the human genome and the concept of common heritage," *Journal of Medicine and Philosophy*, vol. 23, no. 3, pp. 234–6. (Discusses the UNESCO declaration on the human genome, integrity of "persons," and the nature of a common heritage.)

9   Witek, R 2005, "Ethics and patentability in biotechnology," *Science and Engineering Ethics*, vol. 11, pp. 105–11. (Describes protections in place in European law regarding privacy and prohibiting human gene patents (as opposed to US law).)

10 Wiesenthal, DL & Weiner, NI 1996, "Privacy and the human genome project," *Ethics and Behavior*, vol. 6, no. 3, pp. 189–201.

11 Tavani, HT 2004 "Genomic research and data-mining technology: implications for personal privacy and informed consent," *Ethics and Information Technology*, vol. 6, pp. 15–28.

12 Sass, HM 1998, "Introduction: why protect the human genome?" *Journal of Medicine and Philosophy*, vol. 23, no. 3, pp. 227–33.

INDEX

airspace ownership, 131–2
anencephaly, and issues of
        personhood, 159–60
animals
    experimentation, 71–2
    and patents, 87–8
Apache, 148
APBiotech, 149
Apriori Foundations of the Civil Law
        (Reinach), 42
Aristotle, 50
autonomy
    legal perspectives, 84–5
    and ownership, 33–4
    and property, 84–5
Avery, O. *et al.*, 53–4

Bayer Group, AG., 149
Bayh-Dole Act, 140–1, 142–3
Beadle, George and Tatum, Edward,
        56
Bell Labs, 142
Bergy, Michael, 86
bio-banks, 50
BiOS initiative, 150
"biotech revolution", 140–41
    role of HGP, 141–3
body parts
    and autonomy, 85

and ownership, 88–90, 127
    property rights, 32
    see also tissue donations
Boveri, Theodor, 53
Bristol–Meyers Squibb, Co., 149
Bush, Vannavar, 139

Cairnes, John, 55
Canavan's disease, 93–4
capacity and personhood, 161
Carothers, Elinor, 53
Catalona case *see Washington*
        University v. Catalona (E.D.
        Missouri 2006)
Celera Corp, 21, 26, 90–91, 99, 142–3
cell nucleus, 25
CERN, 140
Chakrabarty case *see Diamond v.*
        Chakrabarty (447 U.S. 303
        [1980])
Chargaff, Erwin, 54
China, bio-prospecting regulation, 152
classical genetics, 50–52
clinical trials
    tissue donations, 94–6, 96–100,
        165–7
    donor safeguards, 166–7
CNVs *see* copy-number variants,
        (CNVs)

Coase, Ronald, 144–5
"code" analogies, 25
codons, 25, 58
the Commons paradigm, 29–30, 126–7, 129–34
    background and legal origins, 129–30
    by choice, 130–31
    by necessity, 131–2
    and DNA, 133–6
consent issues, 166–8
copy–number variants (CNVs), 33, 73
copyright
    cf. patent, 109–11
    extensions, 146
creating new life forms, 161–2
Crichton, Michael, 161–2

Darwin, Charles, 50, 69
Dawkins, Richard, 73
deCODE, 151–2
Diamond v. Chakrabarty (447 U.S. 303 [1980]), 26, 86, 113, 121
differentiation, 59–60
discovery and patents, 108–9, 113, 121
disease patents, 93–6
DNA (deoxyribonucleic acid), 20, 24–6
    biochemical structure, 49, 55
        discovery, 54–5
    metabolic functions, 57–8
    ownership and protection status, 32, 127–8, 133–6
        and copyright, 128
        ontological groundedness, 43–5, 136
    as shared resource, 128, 133–6
    relationship to individuals, 32, 33–4
    see also gene patents; genome ownership
DNA sampling practices, 50
The Double Helix (Watson), 55

economics of genome ownership, 34–5, 137–8
    "big business" interests, 141–3
    marketplace for genes, 143–6
    open sources and free markets, 146–8
environmental influences, 33–4, 61, 64–5
epigenetics, 33–4, 64–5
Estonia, 167
ethical theory and ontology, 35–7, 40–8
    approaches, 40–41
    groundedness as empirical measure, 41–3
    human DNA as exceptional case, 43–5
    ownership of moveables and groundedness, 45–6
ethnic "differences", 81
evolutionary theory, 68–70
exchanges and gifts, 46
expressions, 60–61, 111–14
    and genes, 121–2, 125
    and ownership, 22, 28–9, 107, 110

free markets, 146–8
fungibles, 77

gender determination, 53
gender "differences", 81
gene expressions, 59–60, 112, 113–14
    and "expression", 60–61, 112, 121–2, 125
gene patents,
    evolution and development, 90–93
    case law precedents, 26, 86, 89–90, 91
    criteria for acceptance, 91–2
    extent of ownership, 143–6
    intellectual property law perspectives, 111–14

future directions, 168–70
legal treatments, 26, 86, 89–90, 91,
    101–2
  in intellectual property law, 111–
    16
  possible ways forward, 116–18
opposition and concerns, 26–7,
    102
  critiques, 26–7, 102, 113–14
  impact on innovation, 94, 100
reversing current status quo,
    143–6
national regulation mechanisms,
    149–53
  use of open source devices, 146–
    8, 148–50
uses and applications, 91–3, 142–3
see also genome ownership
gene structure and function, 20, 24–6,
    55–7
information encoding sites, 33
General Public Licence (GPL), 147
genetic determinism, 33–4
"genetic exceptionalism" arguments,
    26–7, 29–30, 35–7
genetic heritage, 162–4
genetics
  classical studies, 50–52
  modern findings, 52–5
genome ownership
  background and justifications, 21
  concerns and objections, 26–7, 102
  economic implications, 34–5,
    137–8
    "big business" interests, 141–3
    marketplace for genes, 143–6
    open sources and free markets,
      146–8
  ethical issues and ontological
    assumptions, 22–4
    property paradigms and the
      common good, 27–9

key concerns and questions, 61–5,
    96–7
  and human intention criteria,
    126
  individuals and information, 61–
    3
  intellectual property law
    discrepancies, 117–18
  need for unique protection
    mechanism, 127–8
key findings, 155–70
  errors in the law, 156–8
  future directions, 168–70
  healthcare implications, 164–8
  infringements of common
    heritage, 162–4
  problems of personhood, 158–60
  property issues, 160–62
key questions and concerns
  "new" genes and gene
    combinations, 114–15, 161–2
  personhood issues, 33–4, 63–5,
    79–81, 158–60
  legal and social challenges, 30–31
    economic and marketplace
      motivations, 34–5
    individuality and personhood,
      33–4
    property concepts and ownership
      of parts, 31–2, 118, 127–8
    unique protection mechanism,
      127–8
  moral dimensions, 134
  potential impact on innovation, 94,
    100
  see also gene patents
"The Genomic Research and
    Accessibility Act" (Becerra and
    Weldon H.R. 977), 22
geographical factors, 69–70
gift donations, 95–6
  see also tissue donors

Governing the Commons (Ostrom), 131
Greenberg v. Miami Children's Hospital Research Institute, Inc. (S.D. Fl.2003), 93–4
Griffith, Frederick, 53
groundedness, 41–3
  defined, 42
  and ownership of ideas, 111
  and ownership of moveables, 44–5, 45–6

HapMap project, 73, 149–50
Hardin, Garrett, 129
Harvard mouse, 88, 115
healthcare implications, 164–8
Hershey, Alfred and Chase, Martha, 54
HGP *see* Human Genome Project (HGP)
histories and life-paths, 75–6
Human Genome Project (HGP), 20–21, 73, 139–40, 141–3
  current concerns, 21–4
human individuals, 79–81
human species, as special cases, 71–2, 72–4

Iceland, deCODE agreements, 151–2
"ideas" and ownership, 43, 102–3, 109–11
  see also intellectual property
identity *see* personal identity
Incyte, Inc., 143
individuality
  genetic mechanisms, 73–4
  and intentional transformation, 78–9
individuals
  and DNA information, 61–3
  relationship to genomes, 74–6
  relationship to persons, 74
  social and legal status, 76–9
    and change, 78–9

cf. species, 68–70
  within species, 72–4
induction processes, 59
Ingram, Vernon, 57
inheritance mechanisms
  Mendelian, 49–50, 51–2
  modern findings, 53–5
insurance industry, 167
intellectual property, 101–18
  concepts and theory, 105–9
    and innovation, 105–9, 109–11
    and justice, 117–18
    problem areas, 109–11
  current ontological considerations, 22–3
    groundedness concepts, 43, 111
    paradigms, 28–9
  current protection schemes, 120–22
  historical development, 102–5
  legal frameworks, 26–30
  as model for genome ownership, 26–30, 97, 111–18
    key concerns and questions, 109–11, 157–8
international legal perspectives, cf. US patent law, 100
international regulatory initiatives, 150–3

"junk" DNA, 72–3
justice
  and ethical theory, 36
  implications of patents on personhood, 81–2
  and intellectual property law, 117–18
  and property rights, 31–2

Kastenmeier, Robert, 88

Lanham (Trademark) Act, 121
laws of nature, and patents, 107–8, 113

Lee, Charles, 73
legal dimensions, 83–100
    autonomy and property, 84–5
    basic roles, 83–4
    concepts of personhood and justice,
        81–2
    early patent cases, 85–7
    ownership of body parts, 88–90
    patenting animals, 87–8
    patenting diseases, 93–6
    patenting donor samples, 94–6
    patenting human genes, 90–3
    questions and concerns, 96–100
        errors, 156–8
        law of personal identity, 97–9
        limitations of patents, 111–14,
            114–16
    US vs. international perspectives, 100
    see also genome ownership;
        intellectual property; property
        rights
life-paths and histories, 75–6
Linux, 147–8

Manhattan Project, 139
mapping the human genome, 20–1,
    73, 139–40, 141–3
marketplace considerations, 143–6
    free and open sources, 146–50
Massachusetts Institute of Technology
    (MIT), 146–8
medical insurance, 167
meiosis, 52–3
Mendel, Gregor, 51–2
mental capacity and personhood, 161
Meselson, Mathew, 55
microorganisms and patents, 85–7
mitosis, 52–5
Moore v. Regents of the University of
    California (51 Cal. 3d. 120
    [1990]), 26, 89–90, 121, 165
Moore, G.E., 47

Morgan, Thomas Hunt, 53
Mosaic browser, 148
"moveables"
    described, 44–5
    groundedness of ownership, 45–6
Mozilla's Firefox, 148
mutations, 57

national regulation of gene markets,
    150–3
natural rights, 83, 110–11
"naturalistic fallacy" arguments, 47
Netscape, 148
"new" genes and gene combinations,
    114–15, 161–2
"new life forms", 161–2
nonfungible goods, 77–8

OncoMouse, 88, 115
ontology
    and ethical theory, 40–48
        approaches, 40–41
        groundedness as empirical
            measure, 41–3
        human DNA as exceptional case,
            43–5, 136
        ownership of moveables and
            groundedness, 45–6
    and intellectual property, 22–3, 28–
        9, 43
The Ontology of Cyberspace, 43
Open Source initiatives, 146–50
    biological applications, 148–50
Ostrom, Elinor, 131
outer space, 132
ownership concepts, 31–2, 129–30
    and the Commons, 29–30, 129–30
    of ideas, 106–7
    and reproduction, 67
    see also ethical theory and ontology;
        genome ownership; intellectual
        property; property rights

Pasteur, Louis, 90–91
"patent stacking" practices, 22
Patent and Trade Office (PTO)(US), 21, 104
patents
    background history, 102–5
    commercial value, 104–5
    criteria for acceptance, 91–2, 114–16
        as products of human intention, 126
    early microorganism/animal cases, 85–7
    human gene patenting, 90–93, 101–2
        case law precedents, 26, 86, 89–90, 91
        limitations, 111–14
        uses and applications, 91–3
    ownership rights, 67, 104–5, 145
        infringement consequences, 92–3
        types and tokens, 66–7
    protection mechanisms, 67
Pauling, Linus, 54–5
Perens, Bruce, 147–8
Perl, 148
personal identity
    and genes, 125
    legal recognition, 97–9
personhood, 25, 63–5, 79–81, 158–60, 160–1
    and gene technologies, 160–62
    and genome ownership, 33–4, 158–60, 160–61
    histories and life-paths, 75–6
    and moral status, 79–80
    relationship to individuality, 62–3, 74
pharmacogenomics, 143
plant patents, 30–31
plants and patents, 86–7

possession, 110–11
    of genes, 118, 123–4, 124–8
    of moveables, 45–6, 122–3
    of non-enclosable objects, 130–31, 131–2
privacy rights, 97–9
promoters, 58
property paradigms, 27–9
    and gene claims, 117–18
    and justice, 31–2
    ownership "groundedness", 44–5, 45–6
    and theft, 42, 45–6
property rights
    existing protection forms, 122–4
        and the Commons, 129–32
        and justice, 31–2
        and possession, 110–11, 118, 122–4, 124–8
    misappropriation scenarios, 90
    types and tokens, 66–7
    see also intellectual property
proteins
    structures, 56–7
    synthesis, 57–8
pseudogenes, 73
PTO see Patent and Trade Office (PTO)(US)

racial "differences", 81
radio waves, 132, 135–6
Raymond, Eric S., 147–8
regulation mechanisms, 149–53
Reinach, Adolf, 42
remuneration schemes, 128
replication processes, 58
ribosomes, 58
"rights" and ownership, 32, 44–5, 145
RNA, 57–8
robbery, 45–6
Roche, 152

sample donations *see* tissue donations
Science – The Endless Frontier (Bush), 139
scientific discovery and patents, 108–9, 113, 121
scientific institutions, development and evolution, 138–41
"semi-conservative" replication, 55
sex-linked traits, 53
sexual reproduction, 49
sickle cell disease, 57
single-nucleotide polymorphisms (SNPs), 33
 mapping projects, 73, 149–50
SNP consortium, 149–50
software
 and the Open Source movement, 146–8
 and property law, 109
species, 68–70
 commonalities, 70–72
 human vs. others, 71–2
 individuals, 72–4
Stahl, Franklin, 55
Stallman, Richard, 147–8
Stanford University, 146–8
Sutton, Walter, 53

Tenenbaum, Andy, 147
theft, ontological perspectives, 42, 45–6
tissue donations, 165–7
 patenting practices, 94–6
  concerns and legal arguments, 96–100
tokens and types, 66–7, 90
 in genes, 124
Torvalds, Linus, 147–8
traits, 49–50, 51–2, 53–4
 dominance and recessiveness, 57
transcription processes, 58

translation processes, 58
23andMe, Inc., 164–5
twins, 62, 74–6

UmanGenomics, 152–3
UNESCO, 100
Universal Declaration on the Human Genome and Human Rights (UNESCO 1997), 100
US patent law, 86–100
 background history, 104–5
 key cases
  Diamond v. Chakrabarty (447 U.S. 303 [1980]), 26, 86, 113, 121
  Greenberg v. Miami Children's Hospital Research Institute, Inc. (S.D. Fl.2003), 93–4
  Moore v. Regents of the University of California (51 Cal. 3d. 120 [1990]), 26, 89–90, 121, 165
  Washington University v. Catalona (E.D. Missouri 2006), 94–6
 Utility Examination Guidelines (2001), 90–91

Venter, Craig, 21, 90–1, 142, 161
Volkin, Elliot and Astrachan, Lawrence, 57–8

Washington University v. Catalona (E.D. Missouri 2006), 94–6
Watson, Jim and Crick, Francis, 54–5
Wellcome Trust (UK), 149
Wilkins, Maurice and Franklin, Rosalind, 54–5
World Intellectual Property Organization (WIPO), 100, 132

Yanofsky, Charles, 57